Never give up!
Eva Mozes Kor, 5/10/11

ECHOES FROM AUSCHWITZ

Dr. Mengele's Twins
The story of Eva and Miriam Mozes

by
Eva Mozes Kor
as told to
Mary Wright

First Printing 1995
Second Printing 1996
Third Printing 2002

ISBN 0-96438-075-7 CB   /   ISBN 0-9643807-6-5 PB

CANDLES, INC.
Children of Auschwitz-Nazi's Deadly Lab
Experiments Survivors
1532 South Third St.
Terre Haute, IN 47802

Dedication

This book is dedicated to all those children - a million and a half of them - who lived and died during the Holocaust. Their only crime was that they were born Jewish. They were deprived of their childhood and denied their families and the love of those families. In this day of Children's Rights, they deserve to be recognized and honored.

It is also dedicated to the children who survived the camps and who have struggled all their lives to overcome the trauma of losing their childhood, their parents and families in a concentration camp.

Finally, it is dedicated to my sister Miriam who died in the summer of 1993 from cancer related to the experiments. I believe she could only have had the disease because of what we endured during Dr. Mengele's experiments. She was my other self. She alone knew what we suffered. She alone survived of my family. I shall miss her terribly.

Last, but not least, this book is dedicated to my son, Alexander (named after my father), and my daughter, Rina, whose childhood was marred by being the children of Holocaust survivors since both my husband, Michael, and I are death camp survivors.

CHAPTERS AND CONTENTS

Special Thanks

In spite of the seeming ignorance of the world, some people seem to have the depths of understanding and human compassion to understand our plight and our mission.

I give special thanks to the staff of the Vigo County Public Library, Terre Haute, Indiana, which has assisted me in so many ways and has been so supportive of what I do; to the late Dr. Werner Lowenstein, Terre Haute, Indiana, who came to my aid and support whenever I needed him; to Mary Wright, my friend and biographer, a former teacher in a small Illinois high school who called me and told me about the information on the twins in Dr. Miklos Nyiszli's book, *Auschwitz, A Doctor's Eyewitness Account*, and then offered to use her knowledge and education to help me write this book; and to Susan Kaufman, my first speech professor at Indiana State University (ISU), my friend and supporter.

Last, but not least, my thanks to the late Andrew Nehf and Mrs. Nehf, good friends always, who so wonderfully filled in the job of "grandparents" to our two children who were deprived of any real grandparents.

It is unusual to find people like this, and I have been blessed to have their help.

PREFACE

I, Eva Kor, was in Washington, D.C., in the spring of 1983 at the American Gathering of Holocaust Survivors convention. I listened to President Reagan's speech in which he dramatically explained to the world his own great pain and sorrow over the deaths of over one million children in World War II. He made it sound as if dying in Auschwitz was one of the greatest things a child could have accomplished in that time. It struck me then as strange that those children who died in Auschwitz have become a symbol and have acquired a greater glory for having died in Auschwitz than we who survived it. At that time, something started in me; some kind of idea was born in me that I had to show those who were glorifying the deaths of children in Auschwitz that surviving it was also deserving of glory and was a tribute to the ingenuity and indomitable spirit of children everywhere.

Just about that same time, I came across a book on

the Holocaust in which the author seemed to show little concern for the people in the pictures which he had selected to use. On one page, there were twelve children pictured behind barbed wire. The explanation told the reader that these children were "murdered in Auschwitz". Yet, one of the children pictured in the extreme right hand corner is not dead because that child is I, Eva Mozes Kor. I contacted this author and told him about his error and explained that these children were photographed on the day of liberation and were not dead. Even though I informed him of his error, no statement of correction has ever reached me and the book is still being circulated with this misrepresentation.

Not long after that incident, I came across another book which contained pictures of children at Auschwitz. In one two-page spread, pictures on the walls of the Auschwitz Museum are shown. When I first saw this section of the book, some very unpleasant memories were brought rushing back to me. I immediately had to close the book; I had such an unexplainable, uncomfortable feeling when looking at those pictures. I remembered an experiment at Auschwitz where we were under observation for hours, at least six to eight hours, and I remembered being most uncomfortable. I knew that those pictures had been taken when they measured the heads of the children, mostly twins, in one of the laboratories. It must have been so demeaning, so unpleasant that I could not remember all the details, yet when I saw those pictures, a flood of emotions came upon me. In those pictures, I am pictured in the upper left-hand corner. Underneath the pictures in the books, the author stated the following: "A wall of exhibits in today's Auschwitz Museum shows what remains of the murdered children - some file photos and a few pieces of clothing."

These are examples from only two books which I have found, but I believe that there are many books on the market that I have not seen that use pictures of children to help dramatize the story of the killings, but they are using pictures of children who were not killed at Auschwitz but survived their terrible childhood there.

I would like, therefore, to write a book which tells of the life of a child before, during, and after Auschwitz. In telling my story, I will be telling the story that will relate to some children who were alive when the Russians liberated the camp on January 27, 1945. Those children with whom I have made contact will be identified. Hopefully, those children whom I have not found will see this book and come forward so that our stories, their stories, after all these long years, might at last be told. I particularly hope to find any surviving twins of Dr. Mengele's heinous experiments.

Most of what can be found to verify those children's survival is found in the films that were taken when the Soviets liberated the camp. I remember thinking to myself that day, "Why do the Soviets want to take pictures of us?" Here we were marching between barbed wires and making a whole show of it while they took pictures. Today, I am grateful because these are the only pictures that I have seen from our liberation. [1]

Many years have passed since 1945. Between 1945 and 1977, I did not give one single thought to those pictures. I don't remember ever even thinking back and trying to remember how I looked or what my thoughts were.

In 1977, the first television series about the Holocaust aired. That series brought back vivid memories of the concentration camp life and of how we survived. Following that, the beginning of recollections of that period of my life began and I began to want to remember. Since then, the flow of memories has never stopped.

From 1977 to 1985 I gave over 100 speeches and I was always cool, calm and collected. Strangely, though, I ended every speech with an unusual statement: "I know that all these things happened to me but I always feel like I am standing up here looking down at this little girl and telling her story." No one ever questioned me about it.

On one occasion, late in 1985, I was lecturing at Indiana State University to Dr. Richard Pierard's class. I was describing my separation from my mother, and I began to sob and sob. I was very confused, troubled and embarrassed because I did not have a handkerchief. I had never needed one before. I cried because I could feel all the pain, fear and horror that I had felt at Auschwitz. I never again ended my lecture by saying that I was telling the story of that little girl. That little girl and I became one. I had suddenly found the child that had been lost at Auschwitz.

Lecturing in public and experiencing the receptive responses of the audience have become my greatest therapy. Little by little, I have remembered more and more. All this happened without my planning it. I deeply resent the many experts and the media people who seem to know everything about us, the survivors. They often say that we feel guilty that we survived and are ashamed about our experiences. As for me, this is 100% incorrect. I was always very proud that I survived. I have never felt guilty that I survived. I believe I did not talk about my experiences because I was not ready to cope with the emotional pain, and my own subconscious was protecting me from the feelings I could not face. By lecturing and always trying to face my pain, I healed myself. I am no longer afraid of any of the memories, but there are still many that are blocked and that is okay with me because my traumatic past no longer cripples me and keeps me from doing whatever I want to do or from being the person I want to be. When people asked me how I survived, I would say I was used in genetic experiments by Dr. Mengele. I don't think that I have gone into great detail except to say that they were taking blood and they were using us in the labs. I talked very superficially about something that almost was not connected to me.

During this same period, I started giving speeches to various community groups, high schools and colleges. On one occasion, a professor at Indiana State University offered his slides that had been taken on his visit to Auschwitz Concentration Camp.

When I went to get them, I asked him if he had, by any chance, seen a movie at Auschwitz which was prepared about the liberation. He said he had. Then I asked him if he had seen any children marching between barbed wires. He again replied yes.

At this point, I asked him if he possibly had the address of the museum, and this man, Dr. Layton, provided me with the address. Immediately, I contacted the museum and asked them the procedure for obtaining the film of the liberation.

Within two months, I had received the film.

My first thoughts were "Would I recognize myself?" and "How did I look that day?" I was really curious by that time.

As I watched the movie, things were moving very fast and the children were marching too fast for me to be able to identify myself because I looked so different from how I thought I would look. Even when I stopped the movie on one of the frames that I wanted to study more closely, I still could not identify myself. So I kept the film on a shelf at home, and really, for all practical purposes, I could not decide what to do with it.

In 1983 when I went to the Washington gathering, there was one big picture - a poster-sized picture - of children in the concentration camp behind the barbed wire. It was a picture from our liberation.

I asked one of the people near-by where the picture came from. That person was Marc Berkowitz and he explained to me that it was developed from a film that was taken at liberation. It was a frame of the film I had at home. I knew then that I could develop the film at home, frame by frame, and try to recognize myself and my sister as well as try to recognize some of the other twins whom I had not seen in 39 years.

Once Marc and I began talking, I found out that he too had been a twin at Auschwitz. It was Marc's desire to have a reunion of all twins, of all the children who were used in the experiments to see how they were doing, how they were getting along and how their health was. Marc had severe spinal injuries and was never in good health because of the experiments.

"Oh, yes, Marc," I said, "this would be wonderful.

I'll gladly go to a reunion. I might even help you a little bit."

When I was walking around at the gathering, I had a sign that I had made out of a piece of cardboard from a package of panty hose and on the cardboard, I wrote in big blue letters "BIRKENAU TWINS EXPERIMENTS - DR. MENGELE".

It was probably the saddest part of my being in Washington at the reunion, walking around, carrying that sign six to eight hours a day, hoping against all odds to meet another surviving twin.

It was very distressing to me that I was asked hundreds of times "What does your sign mean?" People wanted to find out who Dr. Mengele's twins were. Nobody knew anything about us or what had been done to us.

Over the years, Marc was skeptical about our being able to put a reunion together or locate other twins. Although progress was slow, we did achieve a mini-reunion in 1985, the fortieth anniversary of the liberation of Auschwitz.

I have worked very hard to tell the world what was done to us. I have written magazine articles, appeared on news shows, I was even arrested in the Capitol Rotunda (5/6/86) and roughed up by what I call the "Capitol Gestapo" in my attempts to tell the world of the terrible things done by Dr. Mengele to innocent children.

Fifty years ago the world possibly did not know what was going on because there was no one to tell them. But why don't the people who supposedly deal in human stories answer my letters and help us tell the world today? Why don't we get responses?

If I were a Nazi criminal, I would get top billing. If

I had died, I would get acclaim. But, I and about 200 other children survived. I am a victim. Yet, I am ignored.

Children and the crimes against them have been rather easily forgotten because the children are dead. It is over, people say. But, it is not over.

We are alive. We have stories to tell. We were victims then and have continued to be victimized because of what we went through.

The world must know our stories too.

This book is dedicated to two basic premises: one, to get the story out of the children who were freed nearly fifty years ago when the Russians liberated Auschwitz-Birkenau; and, two, to help raise money to fund the search for the children, now adults, who marched out of the camp that day. I would like to get re-acquainted with them and bridge the gap of the years since then. There was life before Auschwitz, life during Auschwitz, and there is life now.

Since those days in Auschwitz, many of us have been engaged in a long search for who we are and what happened to us. Our voices have been unnoticed because we are so few in number and because what happened to us is mostly unknown to the world.

We were not murdered and we should not be identified as dead.

We are here and our voices are clear.

Our thoughts contain many memories of those times, and even though they are the memories of children, they are, nonetheless, true.

They are our voices. They are the voices of the children of Auschwitz. Our cause is the cause of truth. We must find our files and what was injected into our bodies. We must uncover why Israel, United States, Germany and Brazil wanted to, and did, cover up the Mengele case.

I do not want anyone punished. I just want the truth and the data on the experiments. We desperately need and want the information of what was injected into our bodies.

Eva Mozes Kor

CHAPTER 1

Why were the Hungarian Jews the last to be surrendered?

My home was in the village of Portz which was in Transylvania. Transylvania is in the upper north-western corner of present-day Rumania. The village itself was located between Marghita and Simleul Silvaniei. (See figure 1).

In 1940, Transylvania became a part of Hungary, and Hungary agreed to support Nazi Germany. Hungary was an ally of Germany. Its leader was Miklos Horthy. In March, 1942, Miklos Kallay was appointed Prime Minister of Hungary; he was the second in command in the country.

In early 1943, Hitler sent for Horthy and discussed

with him Hungary's obligations to Germany and its failure to take action against the Jews. Horthy insisted that the Hungarian government would continue to try to be neutral and would not pursue policies dictated by the Germans. As late as May, 1943, Horthy and Kallay refused to hand over Jews as long as Germany refused to reveal their fate.

In March, 1944, Hitler again asked Horthy and his cabinet to meet with him; they refused to attend. Because Horthy's position was in contradiction to agreements signed in 1940, Hitler indicated that it would be necessary for Germany to occupy Hungary in order to bring them into compliance.

To keep German troops out of Hungary, Horthy traveled to Berlin for a meeting with Hitler. Once there, Hitler held him prisoner for twenty-four hours - a long enough time period to enable the Germans to occupy Hungary. By the time Horthy was released and returned to Hungary on March 19, 1944, a new Hungarian government under the leadership of Prime Minister General Domé Sztojay had been established. This government was pro-Nazi and much more willing to cooperate with the Germans. This meant that finally the resettlement of the Hungarian Jews - or deportation - could be begun.

Adolf Eichmann went to Budapest and ordered the Jewish population to select a Judenrat (Jewish Council) who would administer the new anti-Jewish laws that forced Jews to register and ordered the Jews to surrender their property. Finally, he ordered the confinement of Hungarian Jews into designated areas.

The designated areas were the six zones or regions into which Hungary and its newly annexed territories had been divided. Jews were rounded up and collected into one central place within each zone (ghettos) and their deportation was begun.

By July 7, 1944, 437,000 of the approximately 650,000 Jews in Hungary had been deported to Auschwitz. The estimates are that 70 percent of the Jewish population of the area known as Greater Hungary was deported, murdered or died under the reign of the Nazis and most of them after March, 1944.[2] While it took nearly four years to rid Poland of its Jews, the process of making Hungary Judenrein was accomplished in nine months.

My family was among the 437,000 deported to death camps.

CHAPTER 2

The beginnings of the Mozes family

My parents were Alexander and Jaffa Mozes. A sister, Edit, was four years older than we were, and a sister, Aliz, was two years older.

My sister Miriam and I were born on January 31, 1935, in the village of Portz in Hungary. In that statement lies one of the many problems that grew out of our experiences. Following the war, in order to get a visa, it was necessary for someone to verify our birth date. Our aunt, with whom we were to make our home after the war, believed that we had been born in 1934. That was the date she gave authorities.

But, my sister and I both believe that we were nine-years-old when we went to Auschwitz in May, 1944.

However, since my aunt told the authorities 1934, we must list our birth date as 1934, not 1935.

My father was one of 13 children, born of two marriages. From the first marriage, there were six children. At the time of our births, all my father's brothers and sisters had left the village of Portz, and my father had bought out their shares of land. We were sole owners of the farm. My grandfather had died before 1940 so I do not remember him, and when I begin my story, my grandmother was living with us on the farm.

My mother was one of two children, and her father owned a huge country store in a larger village. I loved to go there because I could eat all the candy I wanted! He treated us so nicely, and we loved him very much - even though we didn't get to see him very often.

My mother's family was also Jewish, and my mother was very close to her mother. My grandmother was ill with what the Hungarians called "sugar disease"; now I know it was diabetes. She had many problems as a result of the disease and was ill and confined to bed quite often. Mother often went to visit her mother and help care for her; however, after the Hungarian takeover in 1940, she was not allowed to go without getting a special traveling permit which was granted purely on the basis of the regional commandant's mood at the time of the request. They were all deported.

In those days, hardly anybody married outside the faith, particularly in rural areas. My parents' marriage had been arranged, as were most marriages in those days. My mother was twenty-three-years-old - which was really old for the times - when she married my father. Everyone told her that she would have a good life on the farm, but I believe that she really hated it. It was a very difficult life, and she worked very hard.

I understand that my father first fell in love with a young woman from the village where his older brother lived. They became engaged, but she wanted my father to become more religious. She seemed to have a great influence over him. Even though she had no dowry, my father very much wanted to marry her. He began to study very hard and became very religious. At some point, however, my father realized the girl only wanted to marry him for his money, so he broke the engagement, paying her a sum of money to break the engagement and forget the promises he had made.

It was after this that he sent two of his best friends to my mother's village to see if there were any marriageable young Jewish women there. They dressed up in their best clothes and each took with him a stick which had a flower on it.

As my father's emissaries, they would visit the marriageable girls to see if they were willing to see my father. The girl indicated her willingness by taking the flower off the end of the stick. From what I heard around me, it seemed that this practice was followed by all Hungarians and Rumanians.

My mother accepted the flower.

These friends then met with mother's relatives to discuss the relationship - even before my mother had the chance to meet my father, her prospective groom. Once all the arrangements were made, the courtship was begun and the marriage followed. That was when my mother met my father for the first time. My when my mother met my father for the first time. My father was a nice-looking man, and he was quite wealthy. My mother was attractive, but at the time of the marriage, she was considered to be practically an old maid. After their marriage, my father and mother began farming the land which my father had bought from his brothers and sisters.

As the years passed, he became much more religious, almost to the point of fanaticism. Religion had not been important to his family, but he believed that the laws of Judaism should be followed to the letter.

So, actually, religion began to play a role in my life before I was even born.

CHAPTER 3

Description of our farm

The farm on which my mother and father settled lay at the north end of our village. In front of the farm was a road which went down the gentle, sloping hills into the village.

Within the village, on each side of the road, stood neatly-packed houses, each with about an acre of land. The houses - which were owned by the villagers - had gardens and orchards. About 100 families lived in the village. It was very backwards. No one had electricity or running water.

Just about where the road branched and a little to the south was a schoolhouse which the village children attended and where I attended until we were deported. It was a one-room schoolhouse, and all the classes met together. To me, it was a very magical place because I wanted to learn to read all the things that were around to read. We had already learned to read Hebrew at age five because we had to read the Jewish Bible at home.

On the same side of the road, but a few houses farther west, there was a house which the local minister or priest lived in. The church was further on down, closer to the end of town. It was a country church with a little cemetery. We were never even to go there.

My father was always so very worried about our going there. I could never figure that out; yet, if we went near that church, he punished us. In my child's mind, I knew that those people were praying to God, too, and they rang their bells to call people for church services. I didn't see anything wrong with them. Besides, the minister's daughter, Luci, was my best friend. She was really the only friend I had before we went to the concentration camp. We were very good friends, and Miriam and I even helped her decorate her Christmas tree a few times.

I could not, however, under any circumstances, go to her church. I could not even look at it.

I could not quite put it together in my mind why God was going to punish me so much if I went to see Luci's church. I did not dare go. But, I was so curious about how it looked inside that I was almost willing to go into it. But, I did not because I thought that God, as well as my father, would punish me if I did. I really wanted to be a good girl; I did not want to give God too much trouble - or my father.

Our property, as I said, was located at the north

end of the village. It fronted the road leading through the village. It was surrounded by a rock wall which served as a fence for our house and outbuildings. There were two entrances into our property: a pedestrian gate and a larger, two-part gate for wagons and horses. We had a huge front yard which was really more of a farm yard.

To the left of the gates were two huge storage places for corn and wheat. The corn was kept in an open-air type of building. The wheat was kept in a stucco building which had an upstairs in it and also had a cellar. We used the cellar to age the wine we made. Mother also stored the milk there which became buttermilk and sour cream which she churned into butter.

Mother put the milk in ceramic-type containers which looked like huge pitchers - the bottom was wide and the top was wide but the center was curved in like an hour glass. She covered them and then would age the milk for yogurt which was made into cheese or for the buttermilk. After the aging, the top part, or the cream, would be removed with wooden spoons; this could be used as sour cream or churned into a butter. Some of these products we kept for ourselves, but others were sold in Simleul Silvaniei because my father had regular customers there. Too, much of it was given to the many relatives who frequently visited us.

We had a lot of cows. The barn started at the edge of the property and was about 180 feet long and 50 feet wide. It was also a stucco building. It ended where the west end of the house began.

This barn, which was 100 by 200 feet in size, was

divided into three parts: one part was about 120 feet long and the cows were kept there. We fed, cleaned and milked them here.

The next part was about 40 feet long; the horses were kept there. We usually had 4 to 8 horses. If we ever got more than eight, my father would sell one. We had three carriages, usually pulled by two horses, although sometimes pulled by four.

The same horses were used for working, plowing, transportation or leisure travel.

Beyond this part of the barn was the third part where we kept hay. In the fall when the corn was being picked, we would have a corn husking party there. All of the villagers would gather in one place and work one evening to help that person. We shared in this work, just like the villagers.

At other times, we would gather in the barn and beat the sunflower seeds out of the sunflowers. Again, this was just like a party. We would tell all the latest stories and gossip about what was gong on in the village.

In the winter, this area would be used for other functions. We raised our own cotton and it had to be gathered, cleaned, combed, and made into flax. This work was done by the older girls. One custom associated with this that I thought was fascinating was that the parties were held at different girls' houses, and the young men would come and try to steal the thread of their "sweetheart". This was a form of courtship.

The cotton that we made was used primarily for towels and sheets. After the older girls had made the flax, we would have one or two gatherings to make the cotton material.

Because we had sheep, we also had wool. My mother would hire two women from the village to make the wool from the sheep into material. This wool material would be made into blankets or something heavier for winter use. Many of the items made from the cotton and wool were being put into our dowries. My mother believed that with four daughters, you had to begin preparations early. My two older sisters had much of their dowries already prepared. They had been neatly monogrammed and packed away. Ours were about half finished when we were deported. I remember Mother spending a great deal of her evening time working on the items.

We also had dances in these barns. The local musicians would gather in someone's barn, and everybody would join in the fun. People dressed up in the Rumanian national costume which had an apron, which had both a front and back to it and was richly embroidered. The white cotton blouses were long-sleeved and were richly embroidered in the same style as the apron. A vest, embroidered in the same design, was worn over the blouse.

We were never allowed to wear anything like this, however; our clothes were always quite different from the peasants'. The cotton material for our clothes was bought in the city, and our clothes were made by a seamstress in another village.

It was an interesting system.

It allowed everyone to share in the work and the fun. We always shared in the work. In most ways, we were just like the villagers, except we were Jewish and we were wealthier. As far as I could tell, practically everything belonged to us except the villagers' homes. But we did consider them our friends. It was our friendship with these people and the times of shared fun that made it very difficult for me to understand why they let the Hungarian guards take us so easily when they come to deport us.

Our farm was very large and we lived very well.

Actually, as I look back, we were very well off. We did not have a lot of money, but we were land owners and harvested good crops. We had everything we could have wanted.

But, all that would change.

CHAPTER 4

Life in the Rumanian countryside

Our house was a very old house. We didn't have running water or electricity. As I look back, I do not even think it was very nice - but, it seemed to be then.

The house started at the north end of the court yard by the storage building for wheat. It had an outside porch which ran the length of the house. There were columns about every ten feet or so. You could enter each of the rooms of the house from this porch. Within the house, you could also go from room to room without going back outside.

In the southeast corner of the house was the winter kitchen. It was huge or at least it seemed to be to me. I remember it had two beds in it: one belonged to my father's mother, my grandmother, and one had belonged to my great aunt, my grandmother's sister. They both were staying with us when the early restrictions on the Jews began. My grandmother died in 1942, but I do not know what happened to my great-aunt. I just remember her bed was in the kitchen but she was gone.

The winter kitchen had a huge built-in stove that we cooked on. It was always warm there in the winter. Any time we ever got cold, we always went there to get warm. We had the warmth of the room, and we could always crawl into bed with Grandmother. She always provided me with protection from my father when I was in trouble and I was always in trouble.

I remember one day I ran to her, and she said, "It's okay, whatever you did. Come on in here." And, I crawled into bed with her.

She would always protect me. That was the one place to run that my father would not dare try to talk to me or punish me. He respected his mother and he would never talk back to her or go against her wishes. When she died, I really lost the best protector I had.

I remember we had lots of storks which built their nests in the chimneys, and we always knew exactly when summer had started and when fall had arrived by the arrival and departure of the storks. When I was young, I knew that storks were very important, for how could babies be born without them? I was convinced until I came back from the concentration camp that the stork brought the baby. Before we went to the camp, every time we would go visit the neighbor who lived catty-cornered from our house,

she would always have a big stomach. Then a baby
would arrive and the stomach would go down. My
mother would always ask her, "When is the stork
coming?"

"Well, such and such a time," said the lady.

I would wonder, "How does the stork know where
to come? How does he know how to find a lady with
a big stomach?"

Even though the story didn't make sense, I
believed everything my mother said. I just thought
the storks must be very smart!

Between the winter kitchen and the house, there
was a dirt-floor entrance area. Off this area was a
door to the storage place where all the goodies were
kept. There was also a staircase to the attic here.
There were lots of things stored in the attic. We used
to climb up to the attic and play and explore.

One thing we loved to do in the attic was to try to
catch doves. If you removed a brick by the eaves,
you could reach out and grab a dove. We always had
lots of doves, and this game provided many hours of
interesting challenges for us.

My mother loved flowers and the front of the
house had a huge flower garden, fenced in with a
small picket fence where Mother had planted every
variety of flower. The garden area was divided into
two parts with the center part specially prepared for
our holy day, Sukkot.

This festival celebrated the harvest. Samples of all
of the fruits of the harvest were placed in an arbor-
type arch. During this seven-day festival, you were
not supposed to eat inside the house or under a roof.
You were supposed to give thanks for the harvest and
be close to nature. We put benches in there and a big

dining room table was brought out for the week.

In the middle of our garden, arbors had been placed and the plants had grown up over them, providing a tent-like protection for us.

Behind the house was a vegetable garden, about 200 feet long by 100 feet wide. This garden was fenced in by a picket fence too. Looking back, I would describe this garden as big enough to feed an army! My mother canned and stored the many vegetables which grew there and fed us for an entire year. Behind this area was an area where we grew potatoes. Beyond the garden and potato patch, fruit trees, berry bushes, and a grape arbor were maintained.

Mother canned so much that we had a special building just to keep the jams, jellies, tomatoes, pickles, beans, corn, and other things Mother canned.

I especially remember we hung huge bunches of grapes from the ceiling on some kind of hook and had grapes into the winter every year.

Things that needed darker storage like carrots and potatoes were stored in the ground in another area or kept in the wine cellar.

Even though we worked hard and grew most of our food, we never went hungry.

I was to remember these days of plenty later.

CHAPTER 5

My mother, Jaffa

When my mother had married my father, she had been told that she would have a good life. But, she hated the farm and was never happy there. Life was very hard for her there because she had to work very hard.

I remember as a child that my parents argued a lot; my mother threatened, even then - some 55 years ago - to leave my father and get a divorce. I did not know or understand what all this meant; I did understand, however, that my mother was very unhappy. It seemed as if her life was planned from one week to the next, from one year to another.

It seemed as if there were always animals to be fed,

clothes to be washed, chores to be done, food to be cooked or housework to be finished. In addition, Mother was always ready to cook for other people or help a neighbor in need. I hardly ever remember her resting. Sometimes on winter evenings, she loved to go into the first bedroom to read or spend some time alone listening to music on the radio.

Any stranger that went through our village and needed a place to stay would always end up at our house. There was no inn or hotel, and the tavern did not rent rooms. The traveler was always sent to our house. It did not matter what kind of person he was; my mother always made him welcome. If he were dirty, my mother and the maid (while the maid was still there) would see that he had a bath and that his clothes were boiled and cleansed of lice. After the restrictions were placed on Jews in 1942, I remember my mother doing all this herself. The traveler who stayed was allowed to sleep in one of the two guest rooms we had.

Any villager who ever had a problem or needed advice always came to my mother, too, because she was fairly well-educated and very understanding.

She did all this as well as her other many chores. Monday was always wash day. We had no washing machine, so all the washing was done in the near-by river. We went to the river and beat the clothes on the rocks. Before taking the clothes to the river, they had to be boiled in a big kettle until they were clean. The work at the river was only to rinse them. In order to do this washing, my mother also had to make her own soap. In the winter, we did the same thing, but there were fewer things washed. The winter clothes were mostly wool, and I am sure that they must have been cleaned in the city on one of the weekly trips.

Thursday was always baking day. On Wednesday night, we would fill pots, shaped like little bassinets, made out of wood by the gypsies who frequently came by, with yeast dough. (These little bassinets were shaped like little baby bath tubs, and there were times when babies were actually bathed in them, but not in ours because then they would not have been kosher.)

We helped Mother prepare the dough on Wednesday night. She would knead the dough in the container and it would rise all night. She had two or three containers she used: one for white bread or challa (a special twisted bread for holy days), one for every day brown bread, and one for cakes. There were no prepared breads, so we baked for a week at a time.

After Mother would get the breads or cakes shaped, she would use a long metal paddle to place the loaves deep into the oven in the summer kitchen. You could put a lot into this oven; my mother used to bake ten loaves of bread and three cakes at one time.

Part of my mother's work load was created by the many relatives who were always visiting us. Even as late as 1943, relatives would come from the cities to visit with us. They would stay a week or two. My mother cheerfully cooked and baked for the extra people and made certain that when they returned to the city, they had food supplies to take with them.

One aunt who came to visit frequently was Aunt Irén (pronounced Erain); it was with her that we made our home after the war. She was married to a lawyer and lived quite well in Kluj, Hungary. They would come to visit us in a chauffeur-driven car. She

used to go to the Riviera or Paris or Rome for her
vacations before the war.

I remember another aunt was married to a factory
owner and lived in Bucharest. She too was quite
wealthy and frequently visited us. Another of my
father's sisters, Goldie, lived in Kraszna, not too far
away from us; we frequently saw them because they
were often in need of food or help.

My mother was an angel from heaven. She always
had time for us. She took us shopping to Simleul
Silvaniei; she read to us from story books. She loved
to sing and shared her love of music with us. When
she ironed, she sang songs for us to enjoy. We would
always sing when we went places in the buggy. She
opened up many new worlds for us.

Mother was particularly concerned about our
appearances, and I remember, with great pleasure,
the trips to the seamstress's house in the village of
Széplak which was about four kilometers away. The
seamstress lived on the south side of the Berretyo
River and to get to her house, we had to go to the village, cross the bridge and travel back.

I do not know how my mother made the appoint-
ments since there were no telephones, but the visits to
the seamstress for our fittings were always special.
The material for our clothes would be ordered from
the city. We would receive word when it had arrived,
and Mother would dress us up, get the fancy horse
and buggy ready, get a buggy driver from the hired
hands and off we would go. Later, when we were not
allowed to have hired help, my father would take us.

When we arrived at the seamstress's house, she
would show us beautiful magazines with the latest
styles of dresses in them. Our eyes would just about

pop out! My mother would make the decisions about the styles, but I loved to look through the magazines. It opened up a completely different world than what we knew.

Mother would always have two dresses exactly the same made for the older girls and two dresses exactly the same made for us. Their dresses were always a little bit more grown up; they had a waist line while ours were yoked and fuller. Mother liked navy, white and pink for the older girls, and she preferred maroon, powder blue, white and pink for us. We would get measured and would make a date for a fitting. When we returned, the seamstress would have the dresses ready for us to try on. We would each get six dresses per year. They must have cost a fortune because they were all made to fit, and none of them were washable. Occasionally, we did inherit some of Edit's and Aliz's dresses, but with the four years' difference in our ages, the older girls' dresses were a little bit too modern and grown up for us. One of my older sisters was also a bit taller than the other, too, so they had to be altered quite a bit as well. It was these dresses, however, made alike, which saved our lives.

For those times, my mother was a fairly well-educated woman. She was very intelligent, and getting an education for her children was very important to her. At that time, the schools had only four grades in Portz. My mother demanded that my father should let the girls study at the gymnasium and then go on to college.

I remember that after my two older sisters finished grade school, my father wanted them to stop attending school. His argument was that they did not need any more education because they were just going to get married. He also argued that too much education would make them not religious.

"Why? Why?" he said. "They are just going to get married. They can read the Book of Prayers. That is enough."

"My children are going to get an education," said Mother. "There is more to reading than just reading the Book of Prayers. My girls will be educated women."

"I agree," he finally said, "but they must study at home. We will hire a tutor who will live with us and prepare Edit and Aliz for their gymnasium test. Then they will stay just a few days in the city."

My mother agreed. "I will accept your compromise, Alexander."

And, so a fraulein came to live with us. She spoke German and instructed the girls in German, music, drawing, and history. She lived with us during this time, and so we would not feel left out, my mother had her teach us some German and instruct us too. My mother just would not give in to the fact that her children were not going to be educated.

As things got worse, about the beginning of 1944, the fraulein had to leave because she was a foreign Jew and they were being deported.

I do not know what happened to her, but much was going to happen to us.

CHAPTER 6

My father, Alexander

My father was a farmer. We owned just about all the land around the village. I remember that he left early in the morning on a horse, but he did not actually work himself. Many times, we would take him his lunch wherever he was. We would walk if he were working fairly close; otherwise, we would go with a maid in the horse and buggy. Halfway from between our house and the edge of the village, we had three apartments and a house for the servants. Some workmen and their families lived there; they worked in the fields and my father supervised, working only when extra help was needed. My father grew corn and wheat as well as other crops. He often

traveled to the near-by village of Széplak to the
farmer's market or to Simleul Silvaniei to sell crops.

I did not really like my father. I felt that he was
very extreme, particularly when it came to religion.
He always worried that we would not grow up religious enough. My mother would say, "Come on,
they are only kids." But, there were many arguments
about things like religion and school between my
mother and father.

It seemed that I was in constant battle with my
father. I was the most outspoken of the girls. Any
time we needed to ask my father for something or to
tell him something, my oldest sister Edit would
encourage me to be the forward one. Among the four
of us, my oldest sister was a very nice sweet girl, but
not outspoken. I really loved Edit, and she probably
had more influence on me than I realized.

"Go on, Eva," Edit said. "You know that you aren't
afraid. You are the only one who knows how to talk
to Daddy. You do it."

I was so flattered that I would go talk to Daddy
about whatever it was. It might have been a request
to go somewhere or a request not to say prayers at
dinner. Whatever it was, my sister would flatter me
and get me to make the request. So I would ask
Daddy, and I would get spanked and punished
because I dared to make the request in Hungarian
and not in Yiddish which we could not speak which
meant we had to be silent at all the holiday dinners.

One punishment was to shut me in the dark storage area which had been dug out of the ground
where we kept fruits and vegetables as well as
canned goods. It was totally dark in there and this is
where my fear of mice developed. I could hear them

scampering around and eating. I could hear the mice scurrying around in there. Later, in the camp at Auschwitz, I would remember being shut in that room with those mice. I did not like the dark or the mice. I also was made to sit in the corner in a dark room.

I never seemed to learn my lesson. I would forget the punishment of the previous time, and I would be the spokesman the next time someone needed to talk to Daddy, I would fall for the flattery and believe that I was the only one who could talk to Daddy. I would be the spokesman, and I would get punished. This battle between me and my father was continuous.

My father prayed every morning. Living on a farm, we had many cats and dogs, most of which lived in the house at some time or another. Before beginning his prayers, my father would tell me, "Eva, get all the cats and dogs out of the house, so they will not disturb me while I am praying."

"Yes, Papa," I would answer.

Well, dogs and cats are fairly smart, as I found out. I would search them out, but particularly when the weather was cold, they did not want to be put outside. We had two big beds, as I mentioned, in the kitchen. The dogs and cats would go as far under the beds as they could, making it almost impossible for me to get them out.

So, right in the middle of his prayers, my father always heard a big "Meow" which was followed by a cat appearing from under the bed.

My father said nothing until he finished his prayers; then he would call me.

"Eva?" Papa said.

"Yes, Papa."

"Did I tell you to get the animals out so they wouldn't bother me during my prayers?"

"Yes, Papa."

"Why didn't you?"

"I tried, Papa."

"Well, you didn't try hard enough. The cat (or dog) bothered me during prayers."

"I'm sorry, Papa."

"I am too, Eva, because you didn't do what I said. I will have to spank you."

I knew it was no good to protest. I got spanked.

I was truly the black sheep of the family.

I very much disliked my father and believed that he was very unreasonable. The standing joke between us was "You just wait until I grow up. Then you will be small, and I will be big, and I will spank you." It never came true.

My sister Miriam remembers Dad as being wonderful. She talks about how he would put her on his lap and tell her stories. I do not ever remember sitting on his lap; I just remember lying over it to get a spanking.

Another problem between my father and me was that he had wanted a son. Since I was the younger of the twins, he often looked at me and said, "You should have been a boy."

It was not my fault that I was a girl; there was nothing I could do about it. However, he did not have any sons, and somehow he blamed it on me. It seemed that my father believed that everything about me was wrong. He made me feel as if I were not good enough; he made me feel as if I had to prove myself all the time. I always believed that I was a lot better than he realized. I believed that I could, and would, prove myself. Perhaps this is what helped to save my life. It had to have helped me in the camp.

Because my father believed so in Judaism, all of our food was blessed by my father. One of the laws of Judaism is that you can not eat milk and meat together. This belief came from the days of Moses.

In those days when Moses was in Egypt, I am sure that cleanliness was not too closely observed. Many of the meats that might have been available might have been contaminated. Perhaps, at some point in time, people became ill from eating meat and drinking milk at the same meal. Thus, kosher foods became a way to avoid illness.

According to Jewish law, religious Jews are not supposed to drink any milk for six hours, if they eat meat. Additionally, the meat must be killed and prepared in a special way, and no meat from an animal that will not cleanse itself, such as a pig, may be eaten.

Jewish food must also be prepared in kosher dishes. Kosher dishes for meat are those dishes that have not had milk in them; conversely, kosher dishes for preparation of foods with milk are those dishes which have not contained meat.

My father demanded that these rules be followed religiously just as he demanded that we say our prayers. If my mother dropped a fork on the floor, she would have to boil it, and my father would have to say special prayers over it because it was no longer kosher since it had been dropped. Our meat had to be cut by a Jewish butcher called a schecter who would come once a week from a neighboring village. We paid him a certain fee. He would kill the animal, bleed it, then say a blessing over it. It then had to be processed in a certain way. In the summer, we did not eat as much meat because we had no way to store it.

Besides his morning prayers, my father was very observant of the Jewish Sabbath (Shabbot) which began on Friday evening at sunset. On Friday nights, speaking Hungarian at the table was forbidden; we were allowed to speak only Yiddish. However, we could not speak Yiddish, so we were not able to talk after sundown on Friday. To me this was very stupid.

I often wonder, "Why didn't he teach us to speak Yiddish?" But, I believe that my father and mother wanted a secret language that they could talk in so the children would not know what the problems were. Certainly, this seemed to be the case as things got worse in 1943 and 1944. They would frequently talk in Yiddish, sometimes angrily.

In order to say the prayers on the Sabbath (Shabbot) or holy days, there must be a congregation of 10 people. We were the only Jewish people in our village; the next village had about three or four and another village had about eight. The Jews of these three villages formed a congregation. Each year, the meeting place was in somebody's house. One year I remember it was in our house. Early in the morning on Shabbot or the holy day, the people would walk to the prayer house and spend most of the day saying the prayers. They had to walk on Shabbot, and they had to begin the prayers by a certain time.

I loved it when the prayers were said at someone else's house because Father would leave very early. Sometimes, my mother would go with him and they would get one of the neighbor's kids to baby sit with us. We would have a great time. We would close up most of the house and have a picnic in the summer kitchen or the winter kitchen. We would have food, especially the chocolate cakes Mother had made on baking day, play games and just have fun. We were supposed to say our prayers, but we did not say them because Daddy was not there to supervise them. Really, that was kind of nice, free, calm time. Frequently, we played Hungarian Rummy and we often read. We would drink lots of the cold milk with the cakes, and we looked forward to it. After Father finished his prayers, he would come home and ask if we had finished our prayers.

We had to pray for half a day on Saturday until we finished one whole book. I didn't understand a word we were praying. I knew how to say the words in Hebrew, but I didn't know what they meant. I knew how to read them from the time I was six, but the only word I could understand in Yiddish was God because it was repeated so many times.

If we were honest when Father came home and said we had not finished our prayers, he would start and go through all the motions and pray out loud and finish the prayer book. The Saturday Prayer Book had to be done every Saturday, and there were special books for the holy days. I do not remember if my sisters were very conscientious about their prayers; I certainly was not. I tried to get them out of the way as quickly as I could.

It wasn't too long until I was wondering what good all that praying had done.

CHAPTER 7

Life before the war

Life was not very complicated for us. In the winter, we would go to bed when it got dark and rise when the sun came up. In the long winter evenings, my parents would frequently get together with the minister, the teacher, the notary and with their families (which made up the local "intelligentsia") and play cards; they would usually come to our house because it was larger and because there were four of us children. About the only thing we children did in the winter was go sledding on a hill on our property.

Summer was a lot more fun. We would get up early in the morning. My mother was a super child psychologist; she always managed to get us to do

what she wanted. No one ever had to awaken us.
She made it a great honor to hear that we had been
the "best helper" on a certain day. We were willing to
do anything to hear that, even get up early to water
the garden.

We would get up very early in the morning - before
Mother and Father were even up. We wouldn't make
any noise. We had to draw water from the well, then
put it into a watering can and then carry it to the
plants. It took a good two hours to get all this done.
We would water all the flowers and all the vegetables in the two gardens.   I never seemed to get quite
finished.

But, Mother knew how much each of us had done,
and she would reward us with her praise. While we
had been working, she had prepared breakfast.
When we finished, we would all eat together. After
we had cleaned up breakfast dishes, we would all
work together weeding the gardens, taking care of
the chickens and ducks and cleaning the house. Once
a week we had to dust and sweep all the floors.

There were other chores to do, as well. We made
our own paint out of a white chalk-like rock. I know
it was chalk because we could write with it. This
chalk-like rock would be boiled with some water,
some sand would be added, along with some bluing,
and we would use the whitewash to paint the sheds
and outbuildings every summer.

The four of us girls spent a lot of time together. In
addition to playing ball and trying to capture the
doves in the attic, we each had our own garden plot
which we planted and kept weeded. We would com-
pete against each other to see who could grow the
nicest vegetables. All the competition was very help-

ful, and it kept us trying to do better and better.

In many ways, although the setting was fairly primitive, we were greatly encouraged to do better and to be smarter than anybody. We were always expected to be better on any given day than we had been the day before. It was a very healthy atmosphere, actually, and we each worked very hard. I am sure that it is responsible for who I am today.

I remember that we spent a great deal of our time in the summer trying to figure out ways to catch the many doves on the farm. We could eat them, and sometimes did, but most of the time, we just caught them, studied them and let them go.

Often, we would take a container of some kind, prop it up with a forked stick, tie a string to the stick and place corn or wheat under the container. We would gently pull the string with us as we went to a hiding place. When a dove walked under the container to get the corn, we would pull the string and catch the dove. This was a great challenge; the doves always seemed to know what we had in mind.

One job we had - and enjoyed - was to go to the village to buy eggs from the people. Once or twice a month, we went to the village and walked the entire length of the village, asking the people if they had any eggs to sell. We knew everybody in the village and we were sent to buy any extra eggs which my mother used to make noodles. She would dry them in the sun and then we would send them to the relatives in the cities where food was so scarce. I was familiar with just about every dog, child, and person in Portz. However, as things got tougher for us, in 1944, we had to stop sending the noodles to our relatives.

One of my earliest memories of life in Portz was that of the young boy who went through the village, ringing his bell and gathering the cows of the villagers to take them out to pasture for the day. Many times, the cows recognized the bell and just went to meet the boy. At night, he would bring the cows back and each cow would go into its own yard. We had about 12 cows, and he took ours too.

The poorer people did not have cows; they had goats. They used the same system, however, with the goats. Sometimes there were not very many goats, and they would be sent with the cows. If there were enough animals, two boys would take the animals. I do not even know how they were paid for their work, but I am sure they must have been paid something.

Life was very simple for us in this rural area of Transylvania. We had little idea of what was happening in the world.

But we would soon find out.

CHAPTER 8

The arrival of the Hungarian Army

My first memories also include the village crier. He was a young boy with a drum who would walk through the village, beating his drum and shouting, "Hear ye! Hear ye! This is the latest news."

Whenever we heard his drum, we would go out, gather and hear the latest news. It was after such an announcement that our lives began to change drastically.

One particular day the announcement had been a little longer. After getting our attention, the crier said, "The notary asks all of the villagers to go up to the top of the hill to welcome the Hungarian Army."

The time was 1940; I was not quite six. It was early

summer and school was out. This announcement was the most exciting thing that had happened in the village in a long time. Had I known then what was going to happen and the changes that would take place in my life, I am sure I would not have been so excited.

I ran to the top of the hill. Everybody and every-thing in the village - dogs, children and adults - went. Our activity stirred up the dust. As we arrived at the top of the hill that day, we all waited anxiously. There had been lots of rumors. We had heard that the Hungarians were killing Jews and occupying their houses. We even heard they were killing Rumanians.

Rumanians and Hungarians hated each other, par-ticularly in Transylvania. Even though the popula-tion in Transylvania was very closely divided between Hungarians and Rumanians, we were an all Rumanian village. There was not one single Hungarian among us. Our village was run by the notary who was just one of the villagers who acted in the capacity of a mayor. We all felt that we were in great danger of being shot or eliminated by the Hungarian Army. We knew that they disliked both Jews and Rumanians. So, they had two reasons to dislike us.

In a sense, we had been abandoned by the Rumanian Army who had left. They had abandoned us to our fate. That morning, about 6 a.m. we had seen the Rumanian Army withdrawing from the area. Our village was very quiet, and any change in routine was very noticeable. Their noise, as they left, was quite a change.

We did not know officially what was happening. But, unofficially, we knew that the Hungarians would be coming.

It was very strange. There was no fighting. One army withdrew, and another took its place.

There was not one shot fired.

That day, our gathering to welcome the Hungarian Army was an attempt to appease the "Conquering Heroes". It was an attempt to save us from what we thought was coming. My parents did not talk to them; we went because my parents feared for us - for what was coming.

It was exciting to a six-year-old girl, but it was frightening, too.

For weeks, I had heard that if the Hungarians came, they would kill us. The stories were being passed around about what the Army had done to others.

At the top of the hill, people climbed up into the trees and did what they could to see. There was a lot of talk. The movement and noise were exciting, but I was concerned because of the stories. For once in my life, I stood right by my mother and father.

Gradually, far away, we saw a big cloud of dust; something was coming.

As the army approached, I could see a vehicle like none I had ever seen. My aunts and uncles had visited us in their cars, but this was no car. It was some kind of jeep or armored car - I knew I had never seen anything like it.

Behind the vehicle came the soldiers, in their uniforms, singing, "We are Horthy's soldiers, best looking soldiers in the world." This was in tribute to Horthy, the new leader of Hungary. They looked interesting to me, a child, not frightening.

The commander stopped and indicated he wanted

to talk to somebody. Nobody spoke Hungarian
except my father and our family.

"I will speak with you," said my father.

"We will stay in the village," said the commander.
"We need some place to stay."

My father translated for the villagers.

"Is there anyone who will accommodate us for the
night?" asked the commander.

No one volunteered to let the soldiers stay with
them.

Finally, my father said, "We have a large yard and
house; come, stay with us."

And, so they came to our house, the only Jewish
house in the village to spend the night.

The main army units and the officers camped in
our yard. The remainder camped in the village.
Even though there had been a lot of talk about persecution, they were very polite, very well-behaved.

I have a feeling that they knew we were Jewish, but
nothing was ever said about it. There did not seem to
be any problems because we were Jewish - at least
not that night.

That evening the officers ate dinner in our house.
We sat at the table with the Commandant. My mother fixed her best Hungarian torte; it was a rich, chocolate torte with lots of whipped cream. Any time after
that night that we wanted a special dessert, we would
ask mother to bake us what we called "Officers'
Torte".

The officers were delighted with the torte and with
my mother's cooking. They exclaimed that they had
never eaten anything as good and kissed my mother's hand in gratitude. This was a big honor for my
mother who said to my father, "If they are murderers,

would they kiss the hand of a Jewish woman?"

The following morning, very early, they left. There were no remains of the Hungarian Army in our village. I remember my parents talking later about them.

"See," said my mother, "there is no truth to the talk that they are killing the Jews. That just isn't true."

"No," said my father. "They were very nice. But why would people tell such stories?"

"I do not know," said my mother. "The stories can't be true. They just want to scare us."

There had been many bad rumors. My father and mother had a battery-operated radio, and they would listen to all the news. They would shut the doors and not let us in to listen. There was a lot of tension in the house after they had listened to the latest news.

Even though I could not listen, I would put my ear to the door and listen to what they were talking about and what the news was. I felt that I didn't dare open my mouth against them, but I was sure that my father was wrong not to be worried, just like when he spanked me for no reason or berated me because I wasn't a boy.

Children do sense when something is wrong, and this was true of us because of the upheaval of the times. I resent the fact that my parents weren't more truthful with us. Even though I know they were trying to protect us from whatever they were worried about, as they found out, there was no way to protect us. Look at what happened.

They surely did not protect us. They didn't want us to know, but we lived to know anyway.

After the Hungarian Army was gone, many changes were initiated.

What changed in our village was the exercise of authority. Until that time, Rumanians had been in charge. Now, Hungarians were installed in the positions of power: the notary was a Hungarian they brought in to serve in that position; the teachers were two Hungarians who were brought from Budapest; the tavern keeper was even replaced by a Hungarian. I remember my parents talking about the new tavern keeper and feeling that he had been placed there to oversee the activities of the villagers.

The official language of the village changed from Rumanian to Hungarian. This was very difficult for most of the villagers because they spoke only Rumanian and were reluctant to learn Hungarian. Hungarian is completely different from Rumanian. They are spelled completely different; there are very few things about them that are the same. I don't remember any difficulty because I was just starting first grade and it was all new to me, and we did, after all, speak Hungarian at home.

Now, it seemed that the people in the village were in much the same boat as we were because the Hungarians hated the Rumanians as much as they hated the Jews. There had always been a lot of fighting between the two nations. Now, in our village, that resentment was very evident.

Some of the villagers learned Hungarian, but most only learned the few words they needed to communicate their needs. They didn't speak it very well, but they could get along. The once friendly notary, who had been a friend of my parents, was no longer friendly. He lived behind the gates of his house and had little to do with the villagers. We never knew what went on behind those gates.

After the Hungarian Army took charge, all the rules and all the laws immediately changed.

The beginning of the end was upon us.

CHAPTER 9

1941-1942

Changes came quickly.

As Jews, we could no longer travel wherever we wanted to; we had to have a special permit. My father had to go to Széplak every two weeks to report. It was like we were on parole. We had to prove on those visits that we were still in the area and that we were not trying to leave. Had he not gone, they would have come after us and arrested us.

We were the only people in Portz who had to do this. Why? Because we were Jews.

That fall of 1940 we were allowed to attend school. We had two Hungarian teachers, and only the Hungarian language was used at school.

The school was a one-room school house. I had not expected to find the books filled with statements of hatred for Jews. The books showed us with big noses and called us "Dirty, smelly Jews". Hatred for Jews was encouraged by all the authorities, and it was taught in the schools.

The law of the land was "Be as mean to the Jews as you can". People saw films, posters, pictures about the "Dirty Jews" and were encouraged by the government to harass and persecute us. There was even a poster on "How to kill a Jew".

The first time I ever saw what we called "jumping pictures on the wall", it dealt only with one topic: how to harass, intimidate and kill a Jew. I was very upset after seeing it. I ran home crying. I knew my mother would be able to explain the horrible things I had seen and heard in the "jumping pictures".

If that is what a government advertises, it is only natural that any child will pick up on it, and he will attempt to carry out the commands. For the Jew, there was no hiding. There was no place to go, no place to complain, no way to avoid it. Jew-hating was part of the culture.

Our math books even had problems in them about killing Jews. I remember one problem: "If you had five Jews, and you killed three Jews, how many Jews would be left?"

School was not easy for us. We were subjected to the usual childish things but there were other things - worse things - which happened because of the campaign against the Jews. Students spit on us and called us names. We were frequently pushed or hit, and we were unable to push back or hit back. We were picked on, goaded into fights where we couldn't fight back.

The other students called us "Dirty Jews" because they knew we wouldn't and couldn't fight back. That made me so angry because I knew I was ten times cleaner than any of them.

Our house was often surrounded by young Hitler youths who would shout obscenities at us. Sometimes they threw rocks or tomatoes at our house. We were hated by everyone and they all treated us as third class citizens for no other reason than the fact we were Jewish.

One day there was a disturbance in the classroom. Some boys must have placed some bird eggs on the teacher's chair. When she sat down, they broke and splattered her new dress.

"The dirty Jews did it," said one child.

"So, did you?" asked the teacher.

Both Miriam and I shook our heads. "No, no, Madame Teacher," we both said.

"Yes, they did," screamed the other kids. "They did it. We saw them."

She just accepted it. She didn't investigate, she didn't listen to our denials. She just accepted it. And, she punished us, the Dirty Jews.

"You will have to be punished then," said the teacher. She made us kneel on corn kernels for an hour right there in the classroom in front of the other students.

The worst part of this incident was when we got home.

"Mother," I said as I burst into the house.

"Yes, Eva. Yes. Calm down." Mother said.

"But, Mother, you don't know what happened," I said.

Then I told her about the school incident and how

everyone accused us of doing it and how the teacher punished us without even trying to find out who really did it.

"I am sorry, Children," Mother finally said, with the hurt showing in her voice.

"But, Mother..." I protested.

"Children, I am sorry. We are Jews, and we just have to take it. There is nothing we can do."

I was so angry. I could not believe what my mother was saying. I loved her, and I stood by her, but how could she say, "You will just have to take it."?

The sense of injustice that I felt during that time, the indignation of being punished for something I didn't do and being so completely innocent were all so beyond my understanding at the age of six.

My father's attitude was very much the same.

"Don't rock the boat," he said. "You will only make more problems for yourself."

"But...." I protested.

"For 2,000 years the Jews have believed that if we try to get along, we will survive," he went on. "We must obey. Somehow we will survive!"

I was not satisfied. I wanted my father to do something about it.

"But, Daddy, they punished us. We didn't do anything. Why are they doing this?"

"Because we are Jews, Eva. Because we are Jews."

And, that was it. No matter how much I complained, he did nothing.

"Ignore it," Mother said.

"Ignore it," Father said. "Pretend it did not happen."

I could not do this. I could not ignore it. I wanted my father to do something about it. Most children expect their parents to stand up for them and I was no different. But, both my mother and father said, "Child, I am very sorry. There is not anything we can do."

Under these conditions, the years of 1941 and 1942 passed. Although there were some minor changes in our situation, life continued much the same except for the Jews who came to sleep and eat at our house.

During this period, we had many visitors who stayed with us. They ate with us and many stayed in our barn. They were all Hungarian Jews from Budapest who had been placed on forced labor details.

At that time, there were no camps for forced laborers. The Jews were often taken off the streets and driven away in trucks, sometimes never to go home again. They were brought out into the countryside to work on the railroad tracks to improve them for the transporting of war materials. They also worked on near-by roads.

Even though they had to sleep outdoors and worked long, hard hours, these conditions were better than any labor camp they had heard about. We helped to feed them and care for them. As long as they got to work on time, no one complained.

Their wives came from Budapest to stay with us too and to visit their husbands. Besides these people, we also had relatives and friends who were suffering in the big cities. In return for our hospitality, they would often bring us books or dolls. The two dolls in the family picture (Illustration 1) were given to us by one of the wives of the laborers.

I especially liked the books which they brought. All of us liked reading, and we could no longer travel

anywhere to buy books. By 1943, I could finish a
book in one day. Books were a very good escape
from what was going on, and I was fascinated with
the places talked about in the books. It was a whole
new world for me and a world where Jews were not
accused of things they didn't do.

In 1942, we became subject to the law that said that
Jews could not hire Aryans and Christians. We had
to let our maids go, as well as the farm workers. At
that time, my father began to allow the farmers in the
village to work the land under a feudalistic-type
arrangement.

These men would work the land and when harvest
came, they would bring the harvest to the court yard
to be divided between them and my father. They
would bring some kind of special sheet or ground
cover and spread it out on the court yard. Then, they
would divide the crop, whatever it was, by giving us
two parts and keeping one part for themselves. We
helped to supervise the distribution as the farmers
divided the beans, potatoes, corn, peas, and other
vegetables that had been grown on our land. At least,
we still had plenty to eat.

After 1942, our travel was also restricted. My
mother could no longer get passes to travel to see her
mother. Her mother, my grandmother, became very
sick in 1943, and Mother could not get a travel pass to
help. My mother was the only daughter, but she
could not get permission to travel to see her mother.

The day was fast approaching though, when we
were going to travel...not by choice, either.

CHAPTER 10

1943 - 1944

The first part of 1943 passed much like 1941 and
1942. Like most Hungarian Jews, we knew what was
going on but believed we were too remote to be bothered and too few in number for the Germans to
worry about.

In the fall of 1943 we were placed under house
arrest. We had to wear the yellow Star of David on
our clothing. Yellow to indicate what cowards the
Jews were. We were allowed to leave the house to go
into the village, and we were allowed to continue our
schooling. Unlike many Jewish children, we actually
went to school until we were deported.

During all this time, we had a fraulein, a foreign

Jew, who had come to live with us and tutor us. She
had been instructing my older sisters in German, art,
music, drawing and history because they could not
leave to continue their schooling. About the beginning of 1944, she had to leave.

Life for us became very bad in late 1943. There
were many rumors about what was going on everywhere - in Germany, especially. My parents had a
battery-operated radio, and they would shut the
doors and not let us in while they listened to the
news. I would put my ear to the door to try to listen
to what was being said on the radio or by my parents.
There was a lot of tension.

One incident that happened that fall impacted my
own children. Our house was once again surrounded
by a group of Nazi youths who harassed us for hours.

I asked my father, "Father, please go out and make
them stop."

He reprimanded me with these words: "Eva, you
are quite a spoiled child. You just don't seem to want
to understand. We are Jews. There is nothing we can
do about it, so just learn to take it."

I hated the helpless feeling I had, and I hated my
father for not standing up for our rights. I thought
then, and I still think, that children expect their parents to protect them. The only way I can describe my
feelings is that I felt trapped - like you would feel in
an elevator car that stops unexpectedly. You have a
helpless feeling: you want to get out but you don't
know how.

Even after I came to the United States, I experienced trauma from this episode. I would react to
Halloween pranks because it brought back the same
memories and feelings I had when those Nazi thugs

surrounded our house. My husband and my children told me, "Mom, if you just leave them alone, they will go away."

This was so similar to what my father had said — "You will just have to take it" — that I couldn't stop the feelings of being trapped — again.

If my parents ever heard anything on the radio about the concentration camps, it was never mentioned to us. They still used Yiddish when they did not want us to understand. I do not know why my father used Yiddish as his secret language. Maybe as a child he had heard things that he wished he had not heard. I believe now, after raising two children, that we make our decisions as parents based on our childhood experiences.

We could feel that something was happening around us and to us, and while I agree that the children should not be burdened with the problem, it is important that the children should be aware of what is going on. I resent the fact that my parents were not more truthful with us. I know now they were trying to protect us from whatever they were worried about. But, as they found out too late, there was no way to protect us. Look at what happened. They certainly did not protect us. They did not want us to know, yet Miriam and I, the youngest, were the only ones who lived to know. I believed then, and I believe now, that my father was wrong.

But, I did not open my mouth to protest. And neither did anyone else.

My parents should have realized that Hitler meant what he was saying. I know it seems impossible to think that someone could kill all the Jews, as Hitler kept threatening, but my parents should have taken some action to run away - to protect us. I still wonder why they did not believe what they heard.

People in Germany and in all of Europe were aware of what was being said, and in 1944 many knew what was going on. But many did not believe that a leader could come to power and do away with a whole nation of people.

My own parents had fairly good reasons for not being more alarmed. I think they believed, as did many other Jews in small villages, that they would somehow escape the Nazis. They hoped, and maybe believed, that the Nazis would not come to our village. We were too far away.

Also, my father was a very religious man, which was true of most European Jews at this time. He knew from Jewish history that through such tragedies God somehow performed miracles and saved the Jews. I think he was hoping for such a miracle. It is important to note that many people never believe that something bad will happen to them; it is always going to happen to somebody else.

Late in 1943, my mother became very ill with typhoid fever. Another Jewish lady came to stay with us and help us. During this time, my mother was near death. She was so weak that she could not turn in the bed.

My father would pick her up gently — she was so fragile — and he would turn her onto her side so she would not get bed sores. That is the only time I can ever remember that he was kind to her or cared for her.

The Jewish lady was a kind of housekeeper/nurse. She took care of Mother and supervised us as we tried to cook, clean and do everything else that had to be done around the farm. We had always helped a great deal around the farm, so it was only natural that we would assume much more responsibility while our mother was ill.

Mother was in bed most of the winter of 1943 and 1944. She gradually began to get better, but she was still very weak. It was very strange to have Mother be so sick because she had always been so strong. Maybe she could see what was going to happen and didn't want to get well.

I will never know.

CHAPTER 11

Resettlement

In October of 1943, before my mother had become ill, she and my father had decided to act. Their concern for us outweighed their desire to "let things be"

They awakened us in the middle of the night.

"Eva, Miriam, wake up," Father said.

Sleepily, we looked up to see both Mother and Father by our bed.

"Get dressed. Quietly. Put on your warm clothes, your boots. Do not light a candle. Be very, very quiet."

"What are we doing?" I asked, always the inquisitive one.

"Eva, please, just do as you are told," said Father.

We dressed and then went to the kitchen. Only the embers in the fireplace glowed there.

"Children," my father said, addressing all four of us, "we are going to try to get over the Rumanian border. We have decided the time has come when we must leave. You are to follow us. Make no noise."

My worst fears had been realized. All the suspicions I had, all the things I had suspected were now becoming reality. What Mother and Father had said in Yiddish had been concern over what was happening and what would happen.

Single-file, with Father leading the way and Mother at the rear, we left the house.

We walked towards the back of our property which was quite a long distance from the house.

But, as quiet as we were, it did no good. When we reached the back property line, we found a group of Hungarian Nazi youths who were guarding our property and were stationed there to make sure we didn't get away. We were only six Jews. How could we have been so important?

They turned us around and marched us back to the house.

I knew then that there was no escape.

A few months after this incident, one morning in late March, 1944, two Hungarian gendarmes came to our house in a buggy and told us to get enough food and clothing for two weeks because we were being moved to a transportation center from which we would be sent to a labor camp. This was the process known as resettlement.

Of course, the arrival of the gendarmes aroused the villagers' curiosity, and many of them gathered around to watch what was happening. These were the people who had helped us farm and had benefited from our harvest. These were the people who had sold us eggs. These were the boys and girls with whom we had gone to school. Yet, no one, not even my best friend, Luci, said anything or tried to stop them. There were only two Hungarian gendarmes, and it would have been so easy to over power them and free us.

Nobody even tried. No one said even a word that they were sorry.

My mother and two older sisters had gathered some food and some clothing. We were taken by buggy to Simleul Silvanei (Szilagy Somnyo), about one hour's ride away. We were placed in a ghetto with approximately 7,000 other Jews from this area of Transylvania. [3]

Simleul Silvanei was the regional headquarters for that area, the area known as Salaj. This was a very rural area, made up of many little villages. From each village, the Jews had been brought together, under the guise of relocation to a labor camp.

I do not remember knowing any of the people in the ghetto. My father's uncle had lived near by, but I do not remember seeing him in the ghetto. We were to stay in the ghetto approximately five weeks.

Each ghetto was different. Ours was located on the banks of the Berretyo River. We built our tents out of sheets and tried to settle ourselves. We were told that we would be sent deep into Hungary to labor camps to await the end of the war and promised no harm would come to us.

Shortly after we arrived in the ghetto, the commandant ordered us to build our tents out of sheets and blankets. When he saw our tents, he said, "Isn't that

great? Look at the Children of Israel living in their
tents like in the days of Moses."

Every time it became very dark and we knew a
storm was approaching because the sky was growing
darker, the commandant said, "Tear your tents down
and build them on the other side of the river."

Some way from the camp was a bridge. So, we
took our tents down and walked down there to cross
the river. All this time, it was raining. By the time we
had taken down our tents, crossed the river and put
them up again, we were all soaked. No one cared.

The ghetto had no buildings except the commandant's headquarters. During our time in the ghetto,
each head of the family was taken there for question-
ing. The day came when my father was taken there.

Apparently, the Germans believed that he had
some gold and silver. Like so many others who were
taken there, my father was badly beaten. Many had
to be carried out of the building on stretchers by their
relatives.

My father's finger nails and toe nails were burned
with candles. He was supposed to tell them what he
had done with his gold and silver. My father told
them he did not have any gold or silver except for
some candle holders. He told them he had invested
all his money in land. They didn't believe him.

When Father returned, he had black and blue
marks all over him. It took him several days to recov-
er. Why this was done, I do not know. I suppose
they had orders to question each head of the family
and obtain as much gold and silver as they could. It
also seemed that there was some kind of schedule to
meet, too, and the delay required that the SS find
something to occupy its time. [4]

While we were in the ghetto, I do not remember doing much. I did not work. The time there is very vague because I did not have to be responsible for anything because I was still a child. When things like this happen to people, it always takes a while to adjust. I just left it up to others to care for me.

While we were in the ghetto, Mother was very weak. She had never really recovered from the typhoid fever she had earlier in the winter. Being outdoors in the cool air and the dampness did not help her weakened condition.

We were supposed to take food for two weeks and we stayed five. Apparently, as soon as my mother or father realized that we would be there longer than two weeks and realized that we were not going to get any food from the Hungarians, we did ration our food and try to make it last. My older sister was in charge of cooking, and she and my father divided the food. We ate once a day. We had beans to eat, but they were carefully rationed. I remember we got only a little portion, and we could not have any more. I remember some people coming to the edge of the ghetto and throwing in some food. I don't remember if we ever got any of this. For the five weeks we were there, I don't really think that I was ever so hungry that I couldn't stand it. I was never filled, and I always felt I could have had a little bit more food. But, being a child that was always a little on the chubby side (people would often tweak my cheeks), I always tended to want to lose weight, so I could rationalize it - less food means I will lose weight.

My mother was very depressed during this time because she realized that it was partially her fault that we were caught up in this trap. I remember her saying that she wished she had gone to Palestine with my father in 1935 when he had wanted to immigrate. Persecution of the Jews was so prevalent all through the area long before the Nazis came into power. In 1935, my uncle was forced to spend a month in jail. He and my father decided to see if they could immigrate to Palestine, so they had gone to Palestine in 1935 to look over the job opportunities and the country. When he had returned, he had urged my mother to go with him to settle in Palestine.

"Please, Jaffa. It is good there. The country is warm. There are jobs. We can manage," he had told her.

"No, Alexander. I can not go. I can't leave my sick mother. I am the only daughter," she had answered.

"But, why? My brother is there. There will be family there," Father had said.

"I can not move with four small children. What would I do? How would I manage?" she said. "Besides, we are safe here."

"But, Jaffa, we must go now. We can get visas. We must go," said Father.

"I have no desire to live in the desert, Alexander. That is it," said Mother.

And, that was it.

But, in 1944, in her weakened condition and with her worry for her family growing as she became more aware of what was going to happen, she seemed to feel guilt. She became more withdrawn and very weak. Most of the time, she was not able to care for us.

Father continued to pray daily, but after the beating, he too seemed to grow weaker.

We awaited our fate.

CHAPTER 12

The ride to Auschwitz

One morning in early May, 1944, after being in the ghetto for about five weeks, we were told to leave everything behind because we were leaving for the labor camp; we were finally being resettled.

The officials told us that everything we would need would be at the camps and that we would only make the cattle car more crowded by taking our belongings. Nevertheless, my mother and older sisters took some food from the tents we lived in. [5]

I am not sure how many there were in our ghetto. I have always had trouble imagining the numbers of people involved; in my child's mind, anything over 100 was a crowd. I would guess that our ghetto contained between five and ten thousand people. [6]

We were herded into cattle cars. We had anywhere
from 70 to 100 people pushed into a car. Each car was
sealed and labeled. My father was responsible for
our car; if anyone escaped, my father would be shot.
He had to keep the people quiet and orderly. He was
the only one allowed to talk to the guard. I do not
remember that it was a long trip. It seems that we
were only in the car for two days and two nights. My
sister, Miriam, insisted that it was a week, however.
Now, however, after talking to others, I know it took
four days.

We had no idea where we were going. I do think
that most of the people believed that we were going
to a labor camp somewhere. The people were more
than willing to believe this story, looking probably for
some way to hope that the inevitable would not happen. As we were preparing to board, the German
guard had announced that we were going to a work
camp.

"This is for your own protection," he said. "If you
work, you will live. You will stay together as families," he said.

But, I did not believe this was for my own good.
Somehow, even though I was just a child, I knew
something awful was about to happen. I wanted
Father to do something - fight, scream, yell.

"Father," I said. "Father, we shouldn't do this. We
should not go."

"Hush, Eva," he said. "Just do as they say and you
will be okay."

Our train rushed to wherever it was going. We
were given no food or water. It seemed that the most
important project this train had was to get some-

where at a certain time. I realized how quickly the train was traveling when I heard how rapidly the clickety-clack, clickety-clack of the train on the tracks was coming.

People were quiet, resigned.

There was a general feeling that somehow something good might come of this. Maybe we really were going to a labor camp.

Each time our train would stop to take on water, my father would ask the guard for water. Each cattle car had its own guard who was stationed on a platform between two cars and was responsible for shooting anyone who tried to escape. How we were supposed to escape from locked cattle cars whose only window had wire over it, I did not know.

There was no room to sit, no room to stand, not even for little people like me or Miriam. I remember being very uncomfortable. It seemed as if there was a mountain of people in the car. During our journey, one person in our car died. At a stop, my father decided to ask the guard to remove the body.

"Guard," he called. "Guard."

"What do you want, you Dirty Jew?" the guard replied.

"Someone has died in here. Can we remove the body?" Father asked.

The guard laughed. That was his only answer.

I do not remember going to the bathroom the whole time. I remember being so thirsty. During each stop, the guard would throw water in through the little window. My father held a bucket underneath the window to catch it. He caught very little. He tried to see that everyone got some. I got a drop or two, but you could not call it a drink. We were so thirsty that even the sight of water made us thirsty. A drop of two would not even begin to quench our thirst. I did not eat.

At the last station where the train stopped before we arrived at Auschwitz (Osciewim in Polish), when my father talked to the guard, he answered in German. We knew we had crossed the border into German-held territory, and from that time on, we did not really believe there was any hope. A feeling of horror took hold of us. As long as we had been in Hungary, there was some hope that we would go to a labor camp because we knew there were labor camps in Hungary, around Budapest.

A general depression set in among the people in the car. Many people started praying and crying. It became very quiet. There was a heavy feeling, like that before a storm. The atmosphere was very depressed.

But the train kept moving us rapidly to our destination.

Clickety-clack, clickety-clack, clickety-clack....faster and faster and faster. On we went toward an unknown destination. Then the train suddenly stopped.

We did not hear the train taking on water. When my father tried to talk to the guard, there was no answer. There was no guard.

We knew we must have arrived at our destination.

As I looked up, as short as I was, I could see only barbed wire in the window and gray sky outside. Some of the people who were tall enough to see through the window said it looked very desolate. There was a gray pallor in the air, and a smell I will never forget.

Day was just breaking, and my father had to say his morning prayers. He had his prayer book out, and he was trying to figure out what direction was East. Other religious people in the car were worrying about that also. Some of the adults were crying. Some of the children were crying. Many were asking God to help them.

As I watched my father and the other people in our car praying to God, a strange feeling of anger swept over me. It was an anger that I had experienced in the past.

I had felt this anger when we had been called "Dirty Jews".

I had felt it when we were punished for disturbances at school that we had not caused.

I had felt it when we were prohibited from seeing my grandmother because we didn't have a travel pass.

I had felt it when the Nazi hoodlums had prevented our leaving Transylvania that dark night.

I had felt it that day when the Hungarian gendarmes were taking us away to the ghetto and no one spoke up or tried to help us, not even my friend Luci.

I felt it as I watched my father open his prayer book. How could he pray at a time like this?

Father looked around, confused. What was he thinking?

"Father, what are you doing?" I asked, almost angrily.

"Eva, we must say our daily prayers," he answered very matter-of-factly.

"Prayers? Father, we have arrived somewhere and we don't even know where we are. They have lied to us. We are not at a work camp. We have been shut up like cattle in this car, without food or water. And you want to pray?"

"Eva, Eva. We must pray. We must pray to God for mercy," said Father.

"Here in this place, wherever it is, you are still praying. What good is it doing?" I asked him angrily.

"Eva, come. God will hear our prayers," he said. He gathered us around him in a corner of the crowded cattle car. It was the last time I was to see him or my sisters, Edit and Aliz.

We listened to him quietly as he spoke, "Promise me that if any of you survive this terrible war that you will go to Palestine where your Uncle Aaron lives and where Jews can live in peace."

When I heard these words, I knew that what I had suspected since his beating in the ghetto was true: he knew the end was near. I also knew that he had told the truth about not having any gold or silver, for if he had buried any, he would have told us about it at that moment.

We solemnly agreed. We would go to Israel.

Father began his prayers.

"Schma Israel - Hear, O Israel", a Jewish prayer which asks God for help.

Outside, I could hear the German voices yelling orders. My own thoughts were interrupted by the screeching sound of the doors of the cattle car being opened by the SS guards who were ordering everybody out.

"Schnell! Schnell! Raus!"

My life was about to change forever.

CHAPTER 13

Arrival at Auschwitz

What I saw as I approached the door made no sense to me. People were getting off; some were huddling together. The older people were being helped. Some mothers were holding on to their children while other children were wandering around after the long period of confinement in the car, just enjoying the air.

The scene I saw as I left the car was indeed desolate, lifeless, hopeless. It was a terrible place, barren, forlorn. I could see high barbed wire fences. I could see buildings, dark and foreboding. It was overcast and it looked very depressing. Everything was gray and gloomy. My first thought was "I do not know if there is a Hell, but this sure looks very close to me."

The camp which stood before me had been begun on June 14, 1940. The actual order for the establishment of the camp had been issued in April of 1940 after the Germans had penetrated the territory around the small village known in Polish as Oswiecim. Anticipating large numbers of Polish Jews from occupied Poland and Silesia, the existence of a camp in the area had been considered imperative.

In June of 1940, the first transport of Poles to Auschwitz was effected. The camp was then situated on the border between Western Galicia and Upper Silesia. The original site of the camp had been a Polish Army base. Auschwitz I was to be both a concentration camp and the major extermination camp. It contained one gas chamber and one crematorium.

Most of the prisoners sent there were at first used to supply labor for the various factories. In October of 1941, a second camp, Birkenau, or Auschwitz II, was established. It was here most of the four million Jews were gassed, for Birkenau had four gas chambers and four crematoriums.

The first transports began to arrive at Auschwitz in March of 1942. In addition to the two camps of Auschwitz and Birkenau, a third camp, a forced labor camp was located at Monowitz. As each transport arrived, a few Jews were selected for slave labor, and the rest were sent to the gas chambers.

Originally, the groups of people selected for the gas chambers walked the three kilometers or so from the Auschwitz station to the Birkenau camp. In early 1944, a direct rail line was built to the Birkenau camp, stopping practically at the door of the crematoria known as K II and K III.

It was here we found ourselves standing on that fateful day in 1944.

After we left the train, everything went very quickly. As soon as we stepped out, my mother grabbed my twin sister, Miriam, and me by our hands. We got out and lined up, side by side, by the railroad car on some kind of concrete ramp.

The SS were walking around among the groups of people, as if searching for something. It seemed that they had a mission. As I looked around, I suddenly realized that my father and Edit and Aliz were gone.

I never saw them again.

I began to hold on to my mother's hand very tightly when I realized my two older sisters and Father were not to be seen. Then, an SS guard rushed quickly by. He was calling out in German, "Zweillinge, zwellinge."

He came back and stopped in front of us. He looked very intently at my sister and me. We were dressed alike, as always, and we looked very much alike.

"Are they twins?" he asked.

My mother hesitated. Then, she said, "Is it good?"

"Yes," answered the guard.

"Yes," said my mother slowly, "they are twins."

Without a word of explanation to my mother, he grabbed us away from my mother and dragged us away leaving her standing there with her bewilderment showing on her face.

We screamed, we pleaded. But our cries fell on deaf ears.

The German guard dragged us across the railroad tracks, away from the platform where we had been. I remember looking back and seeing my mother, her arms outstretched towards us. Her face showed the despair she must have been feeling.

Then, a soldier began to pull my mother in the direction of the others, and she disappeared into the crowd.

I never saw her again.

Looking back, I am sure that it was the burgundy dresses we were wearing that caught the SS guard's attention. Those dresses, so carefully designed and ordered by our mother, were probably instrumental in saving our lives. In later years, I wondered why my two older sisters did not also attract the guards' attention. They too were wearing identical white sailor dresses with navy blue collars because Mother always had two of everything made, exactly alike. I wondered if they had been mistaken for twins, but in their naiveté, told the truth and thus condemned themselves to death. There was one case that I know of where two sisters, ages 12 and 13, were accepted as twins and survived.

Everything went unbelievably fast — like lightning. I do not know if all the twins in our transport were found as we were or if they were discovered as they went through the selection process. Near the train, the people were quickly being separated into groups. One group had all of the young men and women. One had the children and the older people.

We were taken to the left of the two groups that were being gathered on the ramp. I was just trying to make sense of what was happening. I was half-numb.

I remember crying when we were grabbed away from our mother, but I do not remember crying any more after that. I believe now that when children are

placed in an environment which is so strange and ter-
rifying to them, like Auschwitz was to us children
who were suddenly separated from everything they
knew and loved and were facing death, they have to
mature very quickly. Their childish ways and reactions are quickly left behind. Children who are faced
with life and death so abruptly are no longer children.

That was the day that I lost my childhood. I was
never to recapture it.

In our transport, the SS found seven sets of twins
including Miriam and me. We were all brought to
stand in a group beside the ramp. We were fourteen
children, bewildered, confused, scared. I do not
know if all of the twins were found as we were or if
they were found in the selection process. Some of the
twins who were used in the experiments were already
in the camp and were selected for the experiments.

One mother was brought over to stand with the
group. She was Mrs. Csenghery, the wife of the store-
keeper in Simleul Silvanei. We knew her because we
had shopped at their store. She had twin daughters,
exactly our age. My mother had often talked to her
about the problems of raising twins.

Our group stood there for about half an hour and
was led away before the others left the ramp. We
were taken to a big building which stood near the
barbed wire fence. This building was like a big gymnasium which had been divided into two parts: one
part was occupied by bleachers, the other by showers. The whole process which took me away from my
mother, my father and my sisters forever, including
the time spent waiting, could not have taken more
than 30 minutes or so.

If you consider the mass of people on our train, it

makes the speed with which all this was carried out even more unbelievable. I did not know then that many thousands of Jews were daily being deported to Auschwitz at the same time we were. I did not know that thousands of Jews were being killed every day at Auschwitz. [7]

I think that it is possible that my father and maybe even my two sisters may have been in the column that passed selection. My father was in his early 40's and was in good health. He had worked outdoors most of his life, and he had worked hard, being a farmer. My sisters were also healthy and strong and fell into the right age range. Although Aliz was only 12, she was almost as big as Edit who was 14 and, I believe, could have passed selection. For years I hoped to find them, but there is no record of their names at Auschwitz, no record of numbers being assigned to them.

I do not think that there is any chance my mother passed selection. She looked extremely depressed and she was still extremely weak from the typhus she had suffered during the winter of 1943 -1944 and into the spring of 1944. During our time in the ghetto, she was somewhat withdrawn. She was weak, and I believe that she felt guilty because of what had happened to us.

Much of what was done in the selection process was non-discriminatory, but I believe that my mother did not look strong and would not have given anyone the impression that she would be fit to work.

As we marched away, we were a strange group of little people, each one looking like someone else. We were ordered to undress as soon as we entered the processing building. I knew bad things happened at this place. Hadn't I already been separated from my mother, my father and my two older sisters? I was mentally prepared to believe that this was a terrible place and only terrible things would happen here. I felt numb, paralyzed both in body and mind.

It seemed like a nightmare that would be over as soon as I opened my eyes. Surely, my beloved mother would be there to love and comfort me when I awakened.

But, I did not awaken.

I believe the brutal and abrupt separation from my mother sent me into shock. In such a state of mind, sitting naked in the company of strangers and not knowing what would happen, the waiting seem like an eternity.

Finally, in the middle of the afternoon, our processing began.

I was about to become A-7063.

All the twins were given short hair cuts. Mrs. Csenghery's head was shaved. The "barber" explained that the twins were being given "privileged treatment" - we were permitted to have hair. Within two weeks our heads were filled with lice, and our heads had to be shaved. It turned out that the privilege of having hair was not really a privilege at all.

Soon after the haircuts, we had showers. Mrs. Csenghery was given striped prison clothing, and our clothes - which had been fumigated - were returned to us. It was another "privilege" to have our own clothes, but our dresses had a big red cross oil-painted on the back. I hated that big red cross on my beautiful burgundy dress. I did not believe, even though they told us so, that to have our own clothes was a privilege. They wanted to mark us so we couldn't escape. But, where was I, a nine-year-old girl, going to run to?

As I said, I believed that bad things were going to happen here, and I had made up my mind not to do anything they asked me to do. When my turn came for the tattooing, I began to scream, kick, struggle and fight. I was not going to allow them to do whatever they wanted without at least trying to fight back.

So when the SS grabbed my arm, I screamed, "I want my mother."

"Hold still," the guard said.

"No, I want my mother. Bring back my mother," I screamed.

"You can't see your mother now," they said.

"I want my mother," I again screamed.

"We will let you see her - tomorrow," they said, trying to calm me.

I remember my thoughts very clearly.

"I know that I can't believe them; they just tore us away from our mother's arms, so why would they reunite us tomorrow? There is not very much that I can do about seeing my mother, but I sure can give them a lot of trouble. And, I intend to give them as much trouble as I possibly can!"

So, I kept on struggling, venting my anger and frustration at them.

Four people had to restrain me while they heated a pen-like gadget over an open flame. After they heated the point, they dipped it into ink, then forced it into my left arm, burning the number A-7063 into the outside of my left arm.

Miriam said that in addition to kicking and screaming, I bit the SS guard holding my arm. I do not remember biting anybody. But, I knew in my subconscious that nice girls do not bite, so I must have blocked it out of my mind.

That was only the beginning of my struggle against the Nazis.

CHAPTER 14

The first 24 hours

After the registration and the promise that I could see my mother later, we were marched to our barrack. On the way, we must have appeared as a strange, little group of people, carefully guarded by the SS. We were directed which way to go and what to do. All the guards must have made us look like a group of dangerous criminals.

As we were marched to our barracks, I saw groups of people near the barracks. One group of skeleton-like people was accompanied by SS guards with huge dogs. They were returning from work. They were very pale and thin, and I remember thinking, "They are like walking skeletons."

As we passed the group, one poor soul stepped out of line, saying, "Kinderle. Kinderle." which means children in German.

Immediately the German guards loosed their two husky, well-fed German Shepherds.

"Attack," was the command.

And, attack the dogs did. They ran at the "trouble-maker" and attacked. They literally tore her apart in front of our eyes.

I tried to take it in, and I tried to make some sense of it all.

But, one can not make sense out of senselessness.

We finally arrived at our barracks which was the second one from the end in Camp IIb. The first barrack, I found out later, was the collection center for those who died each day or night after roll call. Their bodies had to be collected in that barracks because if somebody died, the body had to be held until after the next roll call so that the count would correlate with what it was supposed to be. It was then taken to the crematorium. Each day at 10 a.m. some women came by with carts that looked like hay carts. These women prisoners pulled the carts and loaded the dead bodies into the carts. They were then taken to the crematorium and cremated with the ones who had been gassed.

The barrack itself was like a huge cattle or horse barn. It had no windows in the side walls, but there were small windows across the top of the barracks, like dormer windows about ten feet above our heads. The only light was that which came in through the windows at the top of the building. It had a huge barn door that opened out. In the summer, these were opened for air.

Down the middle of each barrack ran a double row of bricks in a bench-like structure. At opposite ends of these bricks was a small warming oven. In the winter, the heat, if there were any, would be vented onto the bricks and would provide us with what warmth we had in the barrack. We also used the small warming oven to cook the potatoes we organized. At the end of our barracks, at the opposite end from the entrance, we had a latrine. Our small latrine - only a three-hole outhouse type one - was another privilege granted to the twins.

The first few days, we stayed in a barracks with adults. The first night, one pair of twins, also Hungarian, showed us around. The bunk beds which were housed on top of each other were stacked three high and two wide. Our bunk was the second bunk on the right at the bottom as you walked into the barracks.

I am not sure how many there were in the barracks in BIIb. After a few days, we were transferred to another barrack because as the transports came in and more twins were found, our group became large enough to merit its own barrack.

After showing us to our bunk, they explained how we were to get our daily food ration.

Shortly after this explanation was begun, all the children rushed to the front of the barracks. The evening meal had arrived and was being distributed.

There was a 2 1/2 inch slice of very dark bread that tasted very much like sawdust when we finally did eat it. There was a brownish fluid every called "ersatz coffee". That was it.

After getting our food, Miriam and I looked at each other. Although we had not eaten any food in four days, there was little doubt in our minds that we could not eat that bread or drink that coffee.

"We cannot eat this," I said to one of the Hungarian twins.

"It's all you will get until tomorrow," he answered. "You had better eat it."

"We cannot eat this. It is not kosher," I said.

They laughed. They began to exchange comments with each other.

"Here, you can have it," I said as I handed over my bread. Miriam offered hers as well.

They took it before we could change our minds.

"We are glad to have the extra portion, but the two you are going to have to learn to eat everything if you want to survive. You can not be fussy. And, you cannot worry about whether or not something is kosher," said one of the older twins.

But, Miriam and I stood firm.

"We cannot violate God's law," I said. Apparently, some of our father's fanaticism had carried over to me without my knowing it.

Looking back now, I was worried about what God would think of me if I ate it. I think that it is somewhat ridiculous now, but the influence of parents on a child cannot be overlooked.

I had really tried, all my life, to be good. I knew that God was very busy and couldn't worry about me or what I did. Still I was worried about what He would think.

I knew God was very busy. I figured him to be a nice, kindly old man sitting up in Heaven with a big book in which He wrote down by your name everything you did wrong. I always worried that He had so much work to do, writing down everything and keeping things straightened out, that I should definitely not worry Him nor give Him any extra work.

My world was so very small then! I determined that I would be a "good kid" so I would not give him too much to have to write down for me. Following that rationale, it seemed best to turn down the non-kosher food. Besides, that is what my Father would have wanted me to do.

After the evening meal, the Hungarian twins and some of the others briefed us about everything that had to do with this camp.

"You are in Birkenau," they told us. "It is part of Auschwitz but is three kilometers from the main camp."

"Auschwitz has one gas chamber and one crematorium. Birkenau has four gas chambers and four crematoriums," someone else contributed.

"We do not understand," Miriam said. "What are you talking about?"

"What is a gas chamber? What is a crematorium?" I asked.

"Come with us," they said. "We will show you."

We walked to the back of the barrack near the door where the barrack supervisor did not notice us. When we got there, we looked up at the sky in the north. We could see glowing flames rising above some chimneys which towered over Birkenau. They were bright red. Smoke covered the whole camp. The smell was terrible.

Even though I was afraid to ask, I heard myself say, "What are they burning so late in the evening?"

"People," one twin said, very casually.

"Burning people," I said. "Don't be ridiculous. You don't burn people."

"Well, the Germans do. They want to burn all the Jews."

"Nobody can kill all the Jews," I said.

"The Germans are trying. After every transport arrives, the chimneys glow day and night," explained one twin knowingly.

"Burning people?" I questioned. "That is crazy. Why would anybody want to burn people?"

Another twin stepped forward. "Did you see the two groups of people that formed this morning? They are probably burning them right now. Only those who can work will stay alive and only as long as they are strong enough to work. The weak, the sick, the old and the young end up in the flames."

I paused. I had seen two groups of people being formed that morning as they dragged us off. In fact, when we had started forward to be processed, the two groups had been standing on the ramp.

I felt the blood freezing in my veins.

I turned my thoughts to my mother, that angel from Heaven, who was so very weak after her long illness and was so depressed over the events which had occurred during the past few days.

I thought of my father, obstinate and stern. I thought of my two older sisters, so like us only older and not twins.

I realized they might all be burning at this very moment because the size of the chimneys, the flames belching forth, the smoke in the sky and the suddenly noticeable odor had confirmed for me, an innocent child, that what they were saying was true. As unbelievable as it was, it was certainly evident to me that they could be telling me the truth.

"They are burning people. They are burning Jews.

They are burning everybody. Don't you know that they are killing everybody that is here?" asked another twin.

I looked up again. The chimneys were extremely convincing. The flames and smoke seemed to dominate everything I saw. The flames were so bright that even though it was night, it wasn't dark.

Suddenly, I angrily said, "What do you mean, everybody? We are not being burned. We are alive."

"For now," one twin said, very knowledgeably.

"Only those who can work or who are of some use are left alive," answered another twin.

All my life I had questioned things. Frequently, my questions had made problems for me, but I didn't care. So I continued belligerently.

"That is ridiculous. We are children. We can not work, but we are alive. Why didn't someone tell me sooner? I have been here one whole day and nobody told me about this."

No one said anything, so I asked, "So, why are we so privileged?"

One of the girls replied, "We might be killed someday, but right now they want us alive because we are twins."

"They use us in experiments," said another girl. "Dr. Mengele does them. They are going to take blood from us. You'll see."

"Dr. Mengele will be here tomorrow, right after roll call. You will find out tomorrow why you were not taken to the gas chamber immediately," said another.

In a trembling voice, I asked, "What experiments are you talking about?"

"Miriam and Eva, I really want you to stop worrying about it," said Lea, one of the Hungarian twins.

She suddenly sounded much more mature than her 12 years. "It is not so bad. I think you better go to bed now. It has been a difficult day for you."

We followed the group back in. Everybody went to bed wearing the clothes he or she had on, so Miriam and I did the same.

We lay in our hard wooden bed on a straw mattress with only a thin, dirty blanket to cover us. I was not only tired physically, but mentally. Yet, I could not sleep.

As I lay there, tossing and turning, I noticed something strange moving on the floor. I began to count: one, two, three, four. My mind thought back to when my father would shut me in the pantry because I had not put all the animals out. The sound was the same. There were mice in here!

"There are mice in here," I screamed out.

"Quiet," someone said. "Those are not mice, they are rats and they will not hurt you if you don't have any food in your bed. Go back to sleep."

I have never seen anything like those rats since that time. They looked more like cats. I did not even know there was such a thing as rats. I had seen mice on the farm because we had always had field mice in the corn and storage bins. In the fall some of these found their way into the house. Too, there were usually some mice in the pantry where my mother had kept her breads. Sometimes when you would reach into the pantry to get something, you would startle a mouse. And, when I was shut in there, I had heard them. But, they were not huge like these rats. These rats lived under the brick bench-like arrangement that ran the length of the barracks.

I remember these rats very well. I have often wondered why so few authors talk about them. I am sure they were everywhere, in all the barracks, because nobody cared about them or tried to exterminate them. [8] This was very close to the experience of someone who has had an unbelievable tragedy in his life and even though he should rest, he can not.

Before going to sleep, Miriam and I went to the latrine which was at the end of the barracks. When we got to the area, I could not believe my eyes, for there on the floor were the corpses of three children, their opened eyes and shriveled bodies mute testimony to the hardships of life in Auschwitz-Birkenau. This picture is just as vivid today as it was that night.

But, I have to admit that sight may be partially responsible for my being here today. Then and there, I made a silent pledge, a pledge that I believe saved my sister's and my life: I would do everything within my power to make sure that Miriam and I would not end up on that filthy floor. From the moment we left the latrine, I concentrated all my efforts, thoughts and being on one thing: Survival.

I now believe that the first day in camp was very crucial to those who survived. If something didn't happen to give them the incentive to live, then they lost the will to live.

Even though we, the twins, were not sentenced to death immediately, that was not enough to survive. I am convinced that had I not seen the dead bodies on that first night that I would not have lived more than a month under the conditions at Birkenau. We were already very thin when we got there; we had not had much to eat in the ghetto. We had lost our parents, our sisters.

We were children in an alien world.

What would have given me the will to survive? The fact that we were not killed as soon as we arrived is just one aspect of survival, I believe. That only gave us the chance to survive.

I wonder, now, if part of our will to live came from our subconscious hopes that if we, the two youngest and smallest of our family, were alive, our mother or father or Edit or Aliz might be alive too. I did not want to think any further than that. The others, particularly my mother and father, must have felt, had they passed selection, that there was nothing to live for. They were separated from each other. By now, they had also found out what happened to the women and children and the old. What would they have to live for? Hope was very important to the people in the camps.

In addition to hope, I now believe that having somebody to count on and who counted on me, somebody who kept me from feeling so alone was another very important ingredient. There were some studies made and most people who survived had a mother, brother, uncle or very good friend who helped organize food or did something to help the other person. Obviously this tends to show that we can not just live in a vacuum, independent of other people.

All the survivors to whom I have talked have left me with the same impression: in order to survive, it was necessary to have someone or some hope to cling to. By the nature of my birth - being born a twin - I had someone.

I thought of my parents, my sisters. I knew somehow that for some reason only Miriam and I had been selected from our family to survive. I knew without being told that my beloved mother had been pushed off into the line that had gone to the crematorium and I knew that my father and my sisters had also gone in that direction.

Somehow, I knew.

Somehow I knew we had only each other. We were alone.

CHAPTER 15

Life begins in Auschwitz

The next morning when we got up, we had to stand in front of the barracks for roll call. It was not even light when they woke us. It did not matter if you were one-year-old or two-years-old or 15-years old, you had to stand for roll call - winter, summer, rain or shine. There were no excuses. Even the dead were brought to roll call. That was the just the way each day started.

After roll call, we went back into the barracks. We had to straighten up the place. Then we lined up for Dr. Mengele's visit to his twins. Everybody stood like a statue, not daring to move or breathe.

This was to be my first sight of Dr. Josef Mengele.

Everybody was extremely petrified of his arrival. Although I learned later that this was the man who passed judgment on the arrivals on the ramp, I had not seen him the day before. But, when he arrived, I remember thinking, "What a handsome man."

Mengele was, indeed, handsome. Dressed immaculately, he entered with an entourage of SS and other supervisors. Surrounding him was an aura that this man could - and would - do anything. The same feeling prevailed every time he appeared. My first impression of him, however, was marred by what happened next.

"Why did these children die?" he screamed at the adults in our barracks when he saw the dead children. "I can not afford to lose even one child." Mengele knew exactly how many twins there were in each barrack, and he became enraged if one died - for whatever reason.

I immediately sensed that he did want us alive, for whatever reason. I was not aware then that some of us would die in his experiments to further the Master Race. Our routine for the next few months established itself that day.

After roll call and the inspection by Dr. Mengele and his entourage, we received our morning food ration. Our food was very poor, exactly the same ration, I think, that the other prisoners received. Some people think we received special treatment. We did get to keep our own clothes, for example, and we didn't have to work. But, I don't believe we got more food or any better treatment otherwise. We did not receive extra food rations or have better living conditions than the other prisoners on the whole. I believe that because we were the only children in the camp, primarily, and because we were separated and not forced to work, that the others in the camp did believe that we received special treatment. This just was not true.

On occasion, the younger children received a piece of margarine and some white bread instead of the brown bread we received, but I did not receive those things. On maybe three or four occasions, when transports came in, the SS had gathered some food from the railroad car and brought it as a supplement, and we received a small container or a little bowl of crumbled cookies, bread or crackers that they had found. This happened only three or four times.

Our morning ration was the ersatz coffee. Although it tasted awful, we learned to drink this bitter fluid which was little more than boiled water. Dysentery - a disease which is a very severe infection of the abdomen, could be deadly. Drinking the boiled water was the only safe water we had to drink because the water was often infested with bacteria which caused typhoid and dysentery.

Each day at noon we received a gooey, very thick, cream-of-wheat-like portion of something. The problem with it was that it was so thick it could not be chewed and could not be swallowed. In meeting with some of the twins in later years, I questioned them about whether they had been able to eat that cream-of-wheat-stuff and they all agreed: it could not be eaten.

In the evening, we received a 2 1/2-inch slice of bread and the coffee I mentioned. On holy days or special holidays, we received some kind of soup at noon. It had beans and peas in it as well as buttons and all kinds of other junk in it. We just removed the

undesirable items and ate the rest. During my whole
stay at Birkenau, we received this only a few times.

The best part of the food ration was the bread
because even though it tasted like it had sawdust in
it, it had some salt in it, and it filled our stomach. [7]
For the period after we ate our bread, we were not
hungry.

As we fell into the routine, I stopped thinking
about my family very much. It was about a month
after our arrival there, I think, that I just stopped
thinking of them at all. I do not know if that was a
defense mechanism of my mind to help me cope with
the harshness and reality of my surroundings or
because, as rumor had it, the food contained some
kind of bromide which, according to many who were
in Auschwitz-Birkenau, made us lose our memory
and weakened our resistance to our way of life. I
knew about the powder because of the rumors
around the camp. [8]

One example of the passiveness which seemed to
take the place of our emotions can be seen in something that happened one day while we were outside
playing.

The twins had been given a fenced-in area beside
our barracks in which to play. We were out there one
day when the death carts were wheeled by. We all
ran to the fence to see if we recognized anybody on
the cart. Suddenly, one of the girls cried out.

"Mama. Mama. It's my mama," she screamed.
She began sobbing uncontrollably as the cart continued on its way. At that moment, we all realized that
our mothers may have also gone by on a cart of bodies. We just hadn't seen her.

We were awed. Nobody said anything to her.

Nobody could say anything. We all felt sorry for her.

"I wonder where my mother is" crossed my mind, I remember. I hadn't really thought of my mother since that first night when I had seen the chimneys flaming. I had become convinced then that my mother was dead, and thoughts of my family or home had rarely crossed my mind. Perhaps this was a built-in protection my mind had created. Or maybe it was the powder they put into the food. Or maybe it was my strong desire not to end up on the bathroom floor as a dead twin.

But I knew I could not worry about death or things I could not control. That was not the way to survive.

That scene, that first night in the bathroom, had given death a new meaning for me but it also made me determined not to end up on the floor of a bathroom or in a cart of bodies. I couldn't worry about my mother or my father or my sisters. I had to worry about myself - and Miriam.

Death meant ending up on that dirty bathroom floor like a piece of meat or lying in a cart of bodies with others who had found escape. That day, death went by on a cart. But, death was not something I would encounter. This will was so strong in me that even later, when I became ill, I was able to make decisions to survive.

I had an unbelievable will to live. I was hanging on for "dear life". The one thing that was important to me was to defeat the Nazis. The only thing to do was to resist death and stay alive.

I knew I would survive. I just knew it.

Illustration 1.
My home was in the village of Portz which was in Transylvania. The village itself was located between Marghita and Simleul Silvaniei.

My mother was an angel from heaven. She was a beautiful, kind person. This picture was taken of her when she was only 14 - the age of my oldest sister Edit when she died at Auschwitz.

Emissaries of my father visited my mother's village and arranged the marriage. I think they were married in 1929. Mother was already 23-years-old - which was very old to get married in those days.

EVA

MIRIAM

EVA MOZES KOR – ONLY SURVIVOR

THE LAST PICTURE OF MY FAMILY
FALL, 1943   PORTZ, HUNGARY

As I walked from room to room to try to find any reminders, any remnants of the life we had once lived, I found one badly crumpled picture. This is the last picture taken of the family. It was taken in late fall, 1943. We are wearing here our burgundy dresses. You can see the apples on the trees. Aliz is on my father's right and Edit is holding his left arm. The little girl beside Edit is Luci, our best friend, the minister's daughter. The little boy in front is a visiting cousin. Today, I am the only family member surviving.

This is our one-year birthday picture. My mother loved to dress us alike, and she would put us in the window and people passing by would think that we were dolls. She was pleased that people admired her beautiful twins. We looked so much alike that she had to put a tag on us to tell us apart.

Summers at home were always filled with the visits of our cousins. Edit is standing in the middle and Aliz is lying on the right. Nobody in this picture survived the camps.

This picture was taken in the fall of 1943. My sister Edit is kneeling down in the front center. The lady in the back row on the right is the teacher who punished Miriam and me at school. The other lady on the left held a position similar to the principal of a school. Aliz is standing between them. Miriam and I are on either side of Edit. The summer kitchen is the building in the background.

My mother and father were very strong people who had worked hard on our farm. Even though my mother had been ill, I hoped for a long time that they had passed inspection and were alive.

This composite was put together from pictures that my Uncle Aaron had when we went to Israel. The picture of my mom and dad was taken in the late 1930's. I had the pictures of Edit and Aliz superimposed on it. That is the way they looked when we were deported. Aliz and Edit were very talented in music and art and would have made wonderful musicians or artists.

The scene I saw as I left the car was indeed desolate. This view of the area where I arrived was taken from the tower of the gates through which the trains entered. The area looks much larger in the pictures than it actually is. It probably is only about 60 feet by 30 feet. It is the one piece of land on the face of the earth where more families were ripped apart forever than any other place.

It was here we arrived on that day in the spring of 1944. When we arrived, our train was on the right side of the platform. Therefore, my mother was dragged off to the right towards the gas chamber and crematorium and we were taken across the tracks to the left, towards the camp.

Once they opened the cattle car doors, a mass of people poured out on the platform. We were bewildered and frozen in place. In this confusion, my father, Edit and Aliz disappeared within a few minutes as my mother was holding onto us.

These two boys who look like twins arrived on a Hungarian transport. They might have been discovered by one of the SS who were running up and down the platform. If they were not discovered by the SS, they would have been taken to the gas chambers. If they were discovered and are still alive today, I hope they will contact us.

Three or four times a week, we were marched the 3 km. or so from Birkenau to Auschwitz I where we entered one of the brick buildings for observation and for different kinds of blood tests and injections.

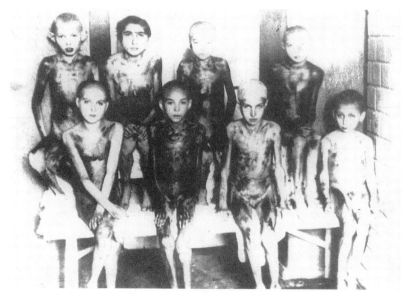

About three times a week, we were marched to Auschwitz I where we were forced to sit naked in a huge room for six to eight hours. We were photographed, painted, measured and marked, and our records were compared. I felt often that I was merely a piece of meat.

I remember that in the fall of 1944 there was a huge explosion. This was the time when the men at Crematorium II tried to revolt against the Nazis and blow up all the crematoria. They only blew up one. It was soon after that the Nazis quit sending people to the gas chambers.

In late December or early January, we were awakened by huge explosions when the Nazis blew up Canada and the remaining crematoria, trying to make sure there was no evidence of what they had been doing at Auschwitz/Birkenau. When the camp was liberated, the Russians found over 1,000,000 clothing articles sorted and ready to ship.

EVA
MOZES
KOR

MIRIAM
MOZES
ZEIGER

AUSCHWITZ LIBERATION
JANUARY 27, 1945

I remember looking at the cameras and thinking, "Are we movie stars or something?" This picture, reprinted from the film the Russians took at liberation, shows Miriam and me as we marched through the electrified fence at liberation. This picture is often mislabeled as children who survived. I Actually, most of the children in this picture are twins who survived the experiments.

When we attended school in Cluj, Rumania, we had school pictures taken which we sent to Uncle Aaron. He gave me these pictures, and I put them together to make a picture of how Miriam and I looked when we were in Rumania after the war. I am on the left.

One of the jobs I had at the Youth Aliyah was milk maid. I did many jobs there, and I would gladly live two years like that again. It was the happiest two years of my life.

PICTURE TAKEN IN AUSCHWITZ
SAME PLACE AS THE LIBERATION
PICTURE WAS TAKEN
DECEMBER, 1991

Miriam and I returned to Auschwitz in December, 1991, and had our picture taken at the same spot where the famous liberation picture was taken by the Russians. Miriam died of cancer in 1993.

In Block 6 of the museum, my picture is still part of the exhibit. The picture of Miriam and me as children walking through the barbed wire is there and this picture is also there. This is the picture that is shown so often where the children are showing their tattoos. This picture was taken in 1995 when I returned to Auschwitz for the fiftieth commemoration of the liberation of the camp.

The following documents verify that experiments were performed on Miriam and me and that we were tested for diseases. They were obtained from the Auschwitz Museum and are notarized for verification.

To Whom It May Concern:

I, Werner L. Loewenstein, M.D., a physician educated in Germany, resident of Terre Haute, IN located in Vigo County, have translated a document from The Camp Physician of The Concentration Camp Auschwitz II.

    The Camp Physician   Birkenau, June 17, 1944
    Concentration Camp Auschwitz II
    (Women Camp)

    To The Hygienic Institute of The Army SS and Police,

    A u s c h w i t z

    Enclosed are throat smears for examination for scarlet fever.

                B l o c k 121

    A list of sixty one names follow-see attached document.

                            Signed by The Camp Physician
                            Concentration Camp Auschwitz II
                            Mengele(looks like his signature)
                            SS Sub Storm Leader

I certify that I have translated the above from the attached documents, and that this is an accurate and true representation of what is contained therein.

Werner L. Loewenstein
Werner L. Loewenstein

State of Indiana
County of Vigo

Before me, the undersigned, a Notary Public in and for said County and State, this 18th day of April 1935 Werner L. Loewenstein personally appeared and acknowledged the execution of the above translation.

Witness my hand and Notarial Seal

signature
Resident of Vigo County

                        My Commission Expires
                        July 13, 1988

Der Lagerarzt des
KL. Auschwitz II.
(Frauenlager)

An das
Hygiene-Institut der Waffen-SS u. Polizei,

Auschwitz.

19 JUN 1944   Birkenau, 17.Juni 1944.

Anbei werden Rachenabstriche zur Untersuchung
auf Scharlach eingesandt u.zw.:

Block 12:

1.	H.Nr.	158699	Schaschkow Nikolaj
2.	"	149894	Zukow Grigorij
3.	"	77370	Pasenkowa Zina
4.	"	77292	Haschohak Larysa
5.	"	77303	Gluszakowa Wala
6.	"	69214	Kowalenko Lena
7.	"	183968	Titow Wiktor
8.	"	183969	Rawkol Alexander
9.	"	61811	Jukzenko Wiera
10.	"	149856	Murawiew Geniek
11.	"	183961	Kujew Alexander
12.	"	158713	Kesikow Aleksander
13.	"	167284	Sledlewski Anatolj
14.	"	A 5122	Lustig Beate
15.	"	A 7202	Friedmann Olga
16.	"	A 5142	Leniger Helga
17.	"	A 3630	Peterfreud Agnes
18.	"	A 5138	Kohn Eva
19.	"	A 11	Salamon Rozsi
20.	"	A 5123	Lustig Brauer Edith
21.	"	A 3637	Marmorstein Marta
22.	"	A 5419	Zelmanowitz Eva
23.	"	A 3641	Meyder Libo
24.	"	A 7736	Molek Salamon
25.	"	A 12089	Fekete Vilmos
26.	"	A 5121	Lustig B.
27.	"	A 3638	Marmorstein Valeria
28.	"	A 7042	Schrötter Veronika
29.	"	A 7208	Sander Rozsi
30.	"	A 7203	Friedmann Eva
31.	"	A 7857	Csengele Lea
32.	"	A 5129	Sattler Magda
33.	"	A 7222	Hermann Piroska

-2-

34.	H.Nr.	A 7738	Malek Jakob
35.	"	A 5554	Weiss Illi
36.	"	A 7650	Wekerle Bella
37.	"	A 7058	Csengele Judith
38.	"	A 7223	Hermann Ilon
39.	"	A 7055	Rosenbaum Judith
40.	"	A 7710	Schwarz Ewa
41.	"	A 4	Salamon Charlotte
42.	"	A 7733	Gottesmann Elias
43.	"	A 7737	Malek Elias
44.	"	A 7734	Gottesmann Jenö
45.	"	A 7063	Mozes Eva
46.	"	A 7064	Mozes Mirjam
47.	"	A 13202	Goldenthal Aleksandra
48.	"	A 6026	Weiss Eva
49.	"	A 7735	Gottesmann Josef
50.	"	A 5131	Malek Judit
51.	"	A 7199	Blajer Edit
52.	"	A 7059	Löringzi Lea
53.	"	A 12090	Löringzi Andras
54.	"	A 7074	Schick Hedi
55.	"	A 12088	Schick Otto
56.	"	A 12087	Schick Josef
57.	"	A 13203	Goldenthal Ernest
58.	"	A 6027	Weiss Vera
59.	"	A 7054	Rosenbaum Ruth
60.	"	A 5128	Sattler Vera
61.	"	A 5141	Lewinger Rozsi

Der Lagerarzt des
KL. Auschwitz II.

SS-Unterstürmer

To Whom It May Concern:

I, Werner L. Loewenstein, M.D., a physician educated in Germany,
resident of Terre Haute, IN, located in Vigo County, have translated
a document from The Camp Physician of The Concentration Camp
Auschwitz II.

The Camp Physician   Birkenau, August 2, 1944
Concentration Camp Auschwitz II
(Women Camp)

To The Hygienic Institute of The Army SS and Police,
                    A u s c h w i t z .

Enclosed are blood samples for examination of syphilis.

A list of ten names follows-see attached document.

Signed by The Camp Physician
Concentration Camp Auschwitz II
Mengele (looks like Mengele's signature)
SS Sub Storm Leader

I certify that I have translated the above from the attached
documents, and that this is an accurate and true representation
of what is contained therein.

Werner L. Loewenstein
Werner L. Loewenstein

State of Indiana
County of Vigo

Before me, the undersigned, a Notary Public in and for said County
and State, this 18th day of __April__ 1985 Werner L. Loewenstein
personally appeared and acknowledged the execution of the above
translation.

Witness my hand and Notarial Seal

Margaret Jeanne Worrell
Resident of Vigo County

My Commission Expires
July 13, 1985

Der Lagerarztes   10. AUG. 1944   Auschwitz, den   194
SS Auschwitz II.
(Frauenlager)

an das
Hygiene-Institut der Waffen-SS u.Polizei,
Auschwitz.

Anbei wird Blutmaterial zur Untersuchung auf
W a R   eingesandt u.zw.:

1.	Häftl.Nr.	80912	Kohnstein Emilie	
2.	"	80913	Kohnstein Gisela	
3.	"	A 8740	Kirz Edith	
4.	"	A 3626	Weiss Olga	
5.	"	A 7259	Mauschloss Judith	
6.	"	A 5771	Molnar Maria	
7.	"	A 6035	Moskowicz Helena	
8.	"	A 7207	Paneth Sara	
9.	"	A 7063	Moses Eva	
10.	"	A 5627	Weiss Malvine	
11.	"	A 54		
12.	"	A 154		

Der Lagerarzt des
KL Auschwitz II.
SS-Untersturmführer

To Whom It May Concern:

I, Werner L. Loewenstein, M.D., a physician educated in Germany, resident of Terre Haute, IN, located in Vigo County, have translated a document from The Camp Physician of The Concentration Camp Auschwitz II.

    The Camp Physician   Birkenau, August 8, 1944
    Concentration Camp Auschwitz II
    (Women Camp)

    To The Hygienic Institute of The Army SS and Police,

    A u s c h w i t z

    Enclosed are blood samples for examination of Urea Nitrogen, Sodium Chloride, Takata-Ara, and Vitamin C.

    A list of nine names follows-see attached document.

                    Signed by The Camp Physician
                    Concentration Camp Auschwitz II
                    Mengele (looks like Mengele's signature)
                    SS Sub Storm Leader

I certify that I have translated the above from the attached document, and that this is an accurate and true representation of what is contained therein.

Werner L. Loewenstein
Werner L. Loewenstein

State of Indiana
County of Vigo

Before me, the undersigned, a Notary Public in and for said County and State, this 18th day of ___April___ 1985 Werner L. Loewenstein personally appeared and acknowledged the execution of the above translation.

Witness my hand and Notarial Seal

Margaret Leann Wassell
Resident of Vigo County

                            My Commission Expires
                            July 13, 1988

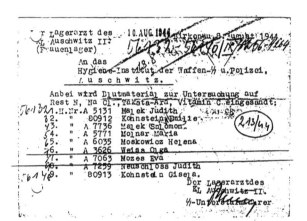

r Lagerarzt des   10.AUG.1944 Birkenau, 8. August 1944
KL Auschwitz II.
(Frauenlager)

An das
Hygiene-Institut der Waffen-SS u.Polizei,
A u s c h w i t z .

Anbei wird Blutmaterial zur Untersuchung auf
Rest N, Na Cl., Takata-Ara, Vitamin C eingesandt:
1. H.Nr.A 5131 Majek Judith
2.   "   80912 Kohnstein Emilie
3.   "   A 7736 Majek Salomon
4.   "   A 5771 Molnar Maria
5.   "   A 6035 Moskowicz Helena
6.   "   A 3626 Weiss Olga
7.   "   A 7063 Mozes Eva
8.   "   A 7299 Neuschloss Judith
9.   "   80913 Kohnstein Gisela.

Der Lagerarztdes
KL Auschwitz II.
SS-Untersturmführer

CHAPTER 16

Routines of camp life

Within two to three weeks of our arrival, we had to have our heads shaved like the other prisoners. Our heads were so infected with lice that shaving them became the only way to control the lice. Thus, the privilege of having our hair turned out not to be a privilege at all. It was kept short after that. In the liberation pictures, we are wearing scarves to cover our heads and it is obvious we don't have much hair. We didn't know that the straw mattress and the dirty blanket were infested with fleas and lice and that even shaving our heads would not get rid of them.

I was also taken back to processing twice to try to correct my number so that it could be read, but I had made up my mind not to be cooperative and I would wriggle my hand so they could not change it. I must have succeeded because I have looked at other people's numbers and they are much clearer than mine.

Once a week, we were allowed to shower, about the only privilege for the twins. It seems that when other prisoners were allowed to shower, it was more of a punishment than a privilege. I have read many times of how they were taken to the showers and were hardly wet before they were marched outside to stand in the cold. In spite of the showers, we were still infested with lice. We cleaned our bodies but we had no way to clean the other nesting places like our beds or mattresses or blankets or clothes.

I remember once when we went to the showers, there were some boys there. I remember looking at them and thinking, "They are so skinny. I'm glad I don't look like that." I didn't know that I did look like that. We had no mirrors, and so in my mind I had not changed. I should have seen a reflection of myself in these boys.

On each trip to the showers, we were given a bar of soap: every week, every trip, one bar of soap. I did think this was unusual because I remembered that my relatives in the city, even before we came to Auschwitz-Birkenau, had complained about the shortage of soap. Yet, we were getting a new bar each week.

At the time, we attributed their allowing us to shower to the German fanaticism for cleanliness. Everywhere around the camp and showers were signs which read "A louse means death to you!" or "Your health depends on cleanliness" or the one in the showers which encouraged you to "Remember your number so you can retrieve your clothes after showering".[12]

My mother had always made our soap, so I knew that the process of making soap involved using fat. There was something about it which did not quite add up in my young mind. It did not make sense that they would give us soap, but no food. What made all this even more strange was the fact that we lived in lice-infested, rat-infested barracks and had no running water. But, who could have, or would have, conceived in his mind that the soap we were being given was made from human fat?

When I did find out in 1946 that this cruel hoax had been played on us, I still had two bars of the soap in my possession. I was in Kluj, Rumania, living with my aunt. The rabbi at the synagogue asked us to bring any soap we had left from the concentration camps to a memorial service the next week. I took my two bars and that was when I learned the truth. The soap we were using was made from human fat.

I developed severe nightmares. I was horrified that I was washing with soap made out of my parents. For years, I was afraid to wash with soap. Although I found it hard to believe and still do, my worst fears were confirmed years later when I found a statement of proof in the book *This Was Oswiecim: Story of a Murder Camp.* [9]

I can not believe that anybody in the whole camp knew that secret. But, I am sure that the Germans did sit back and laugh at the Jews washing themselves with soap made from the bodies of their own parents and relatives and friends. They were just playing another dirty joke on us and having fun. It was a way of life for them.

On one of the trips to the showers, I saw a pile of dishes. I did not have a pot of any sort to cook any food I organized. In camp language, organize meant taking anything that would enable you to survive. It was generally taken from the Germans, but there were instances when prisoners stole from prisoners.

I knew, when I saw that pile of dishes, that I had to get a dish for Miriam and me. I never knew when I did something like that if I would get caught and punished or not. But, I was willing to take the dare and try to get a dish.

We marched most of the time in five's. This particular day I was somewhere in the middle of a row and in the middle of the group. I worked myself toward the edge of the group. I kept changing places with the girl next to me until I had worked my way to the outside of the group. Just as we approached the pots and pans, I took a big leap, grabbed a pot, put it into my dress and marched on as if nothing had happened. Nobody ever said anything to me about it or punished me. If the SS guard accompanying us saw, he never said anything. I believe that they did not see me because they did not look kindly on Dr. Mengele's kids stealing. It was not permissible for anybody, but especially not permissible for us because we were supposedly so "well treated".

A couple of months after we arrived in the camp, my dress was so worn out that I had to be given a new one. My "new" dress was a long, dark gray dress. It was much too large for me, and I had to pull it up around the waist and tie it with a piece of rope. This extra pouch in the dress made it much easier for me to carry our belongings and to hide the items that I organized.

It is the dress that I was wearing when we were liberated.

Our barracks was supervised by an SS guard, a blocova, and a pflegerin or nurse. The pflegerin was short, dark-complexioned, had long black hair, wore glasses and was very neat. We called her "Snake". Her greatest pleasure seemed to be in watching us play her dumb games. She saw it, I believe, as a way to ridicule us.

We had lost, for the most part, any of our childish desires to participate in games or childish things, but we did what we were told. "Snake" had a stupid German song which she would make us stand in a circle and sing. The words meant something like "I am a little black girl". It was the only song she knew or liked.

Someone had to be in the circle to be the little black girl. There was one line in it that said "Da fui, da fui, da fui". When we got to that line, we would rub one finger over the other to indicate a "shame on you" sign.

Later on that fall, the Polish children that joined us taught us another song. At the time they joined us, I wondered why they were allowed to live because they were not twins. I did not know that the order had been given that there were to be no more gassings at Auschwitz. These children taught us a song that was something like this: "Left, right, left, right, we all march together". To this day, it is all the Polish I know.

Apparently, the German pflegerin did not object to this song because we were allowed to sing it as well as her song. I do not remember our other supervisors. The pflegerin was very active and spent a great deal of time with us.

We also entertained ourselves by learning to knit. We pulled pieces from the barbed wire fencing and sharpened them on some rocks. The older girls taught us how to knit. We had a sweater that one of the girls had worn, and we took it apart, salvaging the yarn. Although it was very primitive, we did learn to knit. Each person would get to knit until the yarn from the sweater was all knitted. Then, the next person would unravel the yarn and start all over again. Even today people say that I knit in a "weird way". I wonder if it has to do with where I learned to knit? My style of knitting is no more different than the way in which I learned to knit!

Some of the time we had when we were not involved in the experiments was spent caring for the younger children. We would watch them and try to entertain them. In addition, we would watch the sky for airplanes that would come to bomb Auschwitz and dream about being free someday. Those American airplanes were the only sign that I had that someone was trying to free us. That gave me the hope so essential to survival - to believing we would be free some day.

If that day ever came.

CHAPTER 17

Staying alive in Auschwitz

Three times a week we were marched to Auschwitz to a big brick building, sort of like a big gymnasium. They would keep us there for about six or eight hours at a time - most of the day.

We were never informed about what they were doing; they just did it to us. Nobody ever said what we were given, what kind of shot for what reason we were getting. Maybe some of the older twins were able to find out somehow, but whatever we knew from rumor was all we knew.

We would have to sit naked in the large room where we first entered, and people in white jackets would observe us and write down notes. They also would study every part of our bodies. They would photograph, measure our heads and arms and bodies, and compare the measurements of one twin to another. The process seemed to go on and on. The twins in the photos in the museum at Auschwitz are samples of what they had to study.

After they measured, they asked questions. I remember people in white coats sitting around and taking notes, watching every movement. It went on and on. Measure, measure, ask questions, measure again. Take pictures, compare to charts and then compare to us.

One thing they kept track of was the color of eyes. They kept a special chart of eye colors. They were especially concerned about the size of the nose and other typically Aryan features. During these times, not only we, the twins, were studied. Mengele also studied giants, midgets, dwarfs and people with abnormalities. [11] I guess he wanted to prevent genetic mutation. They must have studied these people at another time. I do know that they were kept in barracks not very far from ours. They would walk freely throughout the camp. Sometimes they even did shows to entertain us.

I am not really sure how many tests there were conducted on the twins as a whole. I have met with several of the twins and I have found out that at least six or seven different types of experiments were conducted on the twins at different times. Although the results were supposed to be sent to the Biological Institute for Research in Berlin, I have never found any records. [12]

The psychological and anatomical tests were fairly simple. In these tests they just wanted to find out how we thought and what our bodies were like.

Always in dealing with us, the Germans were very cold, very matter of fact and very methodical.

Dr. Mengele came into the barracks every day after roll call. He was always very business-like and very cold in his manner. Mengele acted almost like a god. He was very pleasant to us, yet he induced fear just by his presence. Some of the twins have talked about the times that he worked on them. They seem to think he was kinder than the other doctors who worked on us.

I would have to say that, as children, we had some kind thoughts for him because, after all, had it not been for him, we would have surely been condemned to death. We did not have, however, any love, affection or loyalty for him. Nor did he have any for us. The only way I can describe the relationship is in a scientific way. Any scientist who is conducting experiments on a laboratory animal has some concern for the animal. A type of caring develops; a relationship begins. We knew we were alive because of the experiments. We obviously wanted to continue to live. We knew that our fates lay in his hands. Thus, we were his guinea pigs.

There was another doctor involved with the projects; his name was Dr. Hans König. He was tall, thin and had grayish-white hair. He often accompanied Mengele on his rounds; a 20-year-old girl from the camp served as their interpreter. Nobody seemed to fear Dr. König, so he must have been thought of more kindly than Mengele because the nurses and supervisors were very frightened of Mengele. Because of their fears, we were afraid of Mengele too. However, nobody was as involved or as feared as Mengele. I believed this even more after I read the book by Dr. Nyiszli, *Auschwitz: A Doctor's Eyewitness Account*.

Mengele was religiously involved, protecting his findings and treasuring people as long as he got what he wanted. His attitude towards us was like that of any scientist to his control group. And we were a control group - not children, just part of his experiments. Unique only because of the duality of our births.

Mengele had an unlimited supply of guinea pigs in the camp. If a twin died, without a doubt, another pair would come in on the next train so the pair could be replaced. We were entirely under the Germans' control, so certainly we could not do anything to ruin their experiments.

In laboratory experiments, scientists observe, study measure responses and keep records. That is exactly what they did to us. We were the guinea pigs in their experiments. Mengele never hesitated to carry out any experiment that he believed would further his research into the genetics of twins or multiple births.

Our fate lay in his hands.

Obviously, Mengele considered the twins to be a genetic event. He considered the dwarfs and giants to be a genetic mutation. In order to create the perfect race, the Master Race, he had to study twins and the dwarfs and giants. But that was no problem, for he had at his disposal all the specimens he might ever need - in every shape and form.

Even today, none of us really knows what was done to us. Among the twins with whom I have talked, three can not speak because they became so ill from diphtheria germs which were injected into their bodies. They have no vocal cords, and no amount of surgery or care has been able to restore their vocal cords.

The older girls told of being taken to a lab where blood from some boys was transfused into their bodies and their blood was transfused into the bodies of the young boys. Some of the doctors who were working on this project told the young girls that they were going to make them into young men.

One twin had his sex organs removed in an attempt to turn him into a girl. Some girls had their uteruses burned. One twin had so many injections of some kind of drug into his spine, all in an effort to change the color of his eyes, that now he is in constant pain from the deterioration of his spinal column.

I know that some of the twins disappeared, but I was told that they had become very ill. One of the girls that I met in Israel told me that she knew of six sets of twins who went to the lab and she knew by rumor (and rumors were surprisingly correct) that they were killed. [13] Apparently, the experiments were in various stages, and I guess he would choose one of the twins for an experiment. If that twin died, then the other twin was killed.

Most of the time, we were put on a table, our arms were tied down and they would begin.

They would take blood from one arm, and they gave us shots in the other. I tried to ignore the pain, but it was hard because sometimes they inserted another needle before withdrawing the first. I do not know of any nine-year-old who likes shots, and I certainly was no different. Besides, they were not even trying to be gentle. After all, weren't we just guinea pigs?

Once they had finished sticking me, I would open my eyes. I didn't want them to know they were hurting me. I always acted like a little soldier. I didn't want to give them the satisfaction of knowing they hurt me.

As I look back now, I believe that Mengele wanted

to have complete control of genetic engineering. If he wanted to create 100 blue-eyed, blonde men, he wanted to be able to do so. If he needed 100 women, he wanted to be able to do that as well.

During this time, nobody made any secret of the fact that we would be terminated when we were no longer useful. But, living in Birkenau, we all knew that death was an every day part of living. Dead bodies were something we saw everywhere. We knew that fate alone controlled whether we would become one of those dead bodies.

My first initiation to death had come when the SS had their dog kill the lady who fell out of line. Since then, I had seen the bodies of the children who had died in the barracks, the many bodies wheeled by each day on the death carts, and I had even seen the bodies of prisoners who had thrown themselves on the electrified fencing to escape Auschwitz.

We were particularly made aware of our situation by our block supervisor who was constantly reminding us.

"Who do you think you are?" she would ask.

We did not answer.

"You think you are so smart because you are still alive. You are going to be dead before long anyway. We are going to kill all of you," she would say.

Staying alive was the most important thing. As long as we were alive, that was the only really important thing. Nobody ever made a secret about terminating us or telling us we would be killed after the experiments were over.

The formula to survive in a place like Auschwitz was an unbelievable desire to live. I had that desire.

But, it was soon to be tested.

CHAPTER 18

What have they done to me?

In early June, about a month after we had arrived at Auschwitz, we were taken to the lab. As usual, we were not informed about what they were doing to us.

On that day, I must have been injected with a germ of some sort. When they chose me for the germ injection, they knew me very well from the psychological observations. They had to know me very well from the observations they had been making all this time. I am sure the character profiles on us had shown me to be the stronger twin. My sister Miriam had been the weaker one all along and had been easier to work with all along. They chose me, I believe, because I was the stronger one. I believe they felt she would not be as good a subject as I would. If I had died, they would have killed Miriam.

Within a short time, I began to feel very ill. I tried very, very hard to hide the fact that I was ill because I did not want to be taken to the infirmary. It was a known fact that anybody that was taken to the infirmary never came back from there.

I knew that on at least two occasions, one twin had become very ill, was taken to the infirmary and never returned. Then the other twin was killed. I did not want this to happen to Miriam.

The next time it became necessary for me to go to the laboratory, I tried very hard to find some way to disguise the fact that I was so ill.

That was very difficult to do. One only had to look at me to know how ill I was.

My arms and legs were quite swollen, and I was running a very high temperature. I remember being outside in the warm sun. It felt so good because I was shivering from the chills and fever of the germs injected into my body.

I knew I was very ill and I was so desperate to hide the illness that I was afraid to be around the other twins. It seemed that I was even more aware of Death symbolized by the flaming chimneys and the awful smell that covered the area because I was so ill. I could see Death in the flaming chimneys and was even more aware of the smell of death from the crematoria.

Suddenly, the air raid sirens sounded. I was going to be saved!

As the warning for the coming bombing attack was given, as sick as I was, I watched with delight as the SS guards ran to hide. This was the greatest encouragement that I could have had at that moment, for I knew that help was coming and that we would, someday, be free - if we could just stay alive.

I watched as a single airplane came over the camp first, making a huge yellow smoke circle over the camp. It outlined the entire area. We knew they would not bomb inside the circle, only outside.

I looked up to the sky and I saw many airplanes. I knew they were American. I did not even know there was a country named Russia, but I knew about America. My father's sister lived there. The good guys lived there, or at least they had lived there in the "jumping pictures on the wall" I had seen with my mother.

It was a ray of hope in the middle of a terrible time.

These flights over the camp were of tremendous help to the people trapped in Auschwitz, I believe. Without the bombing raids, I would have had no concept of whether the outside world was still there. I had no news; I had no radio. As a child, I had lost all point of reference to the past and the outside world.

Besides, we twins were totally cut off, even from the main group of prisoners.

We were always under guard, for Mengele could not lose his precious guinea pigs.

How long can a child, or any human being for that matter, live and fight for life without hope? Hope is a very important ingredient when one is struggling to live. Those airplanes represented hope.

Looking back, I only wish, like many prisoners, that they had bombed the railroad tracks. It would have at least slowed down the arrival of the trains, even if it had not stopped them.

I believe that other prisoners, besides myself, found

great hope in the arrival of the airplanes and the dropping of the bombs. The bombing scene that I witnessed on that day when I was so very ill was to be repeated many times during the summer and fall, and each time it brought the inmates a new hope of being saved. Somebody out there knew where we were.

That day, the bombing meant that I did not have to go to the laboratory.

But, it only gave me peace of mind until the next visit to the laboratory.

When I went to the laboratory on my next visit, I did not have to worry about hiding my illness. The fact that I was ill was very obvious.

They did not even check me or take blood as they usually did. They immediately checked my fever which was very unusual. I know my fever was very high because I was so hot and trembling; I was immediately taken to the infirmary.

The infirmary was a whole camp with many barracks and was close the gas chambers. My barrack was full of people who were very sick and seemed to be waiting only for death

I was placed in a room with two other twins who were already there. They only had chicken pox, so they were not very ill. Our room was very small but only the two other twins and I occupied it, another privilege granted to the twins.

The other "patients" occupied one huge room which looked like the valley of death. People there were very sick, many near death. They formed a sea of bodies, waiting for death.

That evening we did not receive a food ration. I couldn't understand why, so I asked.

"Why aren't they feeding us? We should be getting our bread," I said.

Vera, one of the twins, explained, "We do not get anything to eat because the people who are brought here are just waiting for their turns to die in the gas chamber."

Her twin, Tamara, went on, "They don't want to waste food on the dying."

I was so ill that I fell asleep, hungry as I was, passing the night very fitfully. Food was the least of my worries.

The next morning, a team of five doctors headed by Dr. Mengele came to examine me, to study my case. They were discussing it and studying it as if it were an ordinary hospital and I had become ill under ordinary circumstances. Which I hadn't.

In their conversation, which I understand because my father had spoken German and we had studied it with the fraulein, I heard Mengele laugh and say, "Too bad. She is so young and has only two weeks to live."

Until I really began to think about all of this, it never occurred to me to wonder how they knew that I had only two weeks to live. They did not even check me over. There were no tests run. Consequently, they had to know what I was supposed to have and what the disease would do to me. They had to know the nature of my illness.

As I listened to them I said to myself, "I am not dead. I am going to prove them wrong and get out of here alive!"

I remember being very thirsty. I would wake up on the floor, having fainted. I was fading in and out of consciousness continuously. The only thing they were doing for me was checking my fever.

They gave me no water, no food, no medicine, no care. I wanted very badly to get some water, even though I knew the water had all kinds of germs in it sometimes. I was so thirsty. I can remember crawling on the barrack floor to the other end of the barrack where there was a faucet with water. Even in a semiconscious state, I kept telling myself, "I must survive! I must survive!"

Of those two weeks, I remember little. In one book, I have read about how the prisoners were given some medications if they were available. I never was given any medications, nor did I even see any medicines. I do not know who got medicine, but it was not I or anyone I knew.

After about two weeks, I started feeling stronger. I became even more determined to be reunited with my sister. Miriam saved her daily bread ration and sent it to me with Mrs. Csenghery after she found out I was often unconscious and had received no food at all.

The block supervisor of the hospital, a very kind German lady, took pity on us children and every now and then would sneak some bread in to us late at night. She would sneak in at night and lay the bread beside me on the bed. One night I woke up and in the semi-darkness I saw her. I could see that she had dark brown hair and was medium-height. I can not remember her features. Once, she even gave us a piece of her birthday cake to share. What a treat that was! Even in a place like Auschwitz, this kind lady proved to me that there were some people who were more humane than others.

Once I began to feel better, I had to convince Mengele and the other doctors that were monitoring my case that I was better and should be released. They came in twice a day and each time took my temperature. Obviously, the five of them were assigned to monitor my disease - whatever it was.

I decided that what I had to do was convince the five of them that my temperature was going down to normal. Then I would be released. Now, how was I to do that?

Vera and Tamara, the two twins with whom I shared the room taught me how to read the thermometer and I developed a simple plan to show that I was gradually improving.

As the so-called nurse would come in, she would place the thermometer under my armpit to get the temperature. She would then leave the room. Since she was really a prisoner like us, she was just doing her job; she was not terribly conscientious about it. I would leave the thermometer under my armpit until it registered my temperature. Then, I would remove the thermometer, read it, and, if it were too high, I would shake it down a little, maybe a tenth or two-tenths. I would then put it back under my armpit with the mercury end extending beyond my arm so it would not register any change.

The nurse would return, read the thermometer and record the temperature I wanted her to record. I had to be careful and do this gradually so I did not arouse any suspicion about getting well too quickly. I was actually able to control how my temperature went down. Actually, I was feeling better - but not as well as the temperature decline indicated.

The plan worked and about three weeks later, I was released. I was very, very happy to be back with Miriam. Even though I was still ill, I was getting better. I knew that returning to the barracks and to Miriam would increase the speed of my recovery.

When I was recovering in the infirmary, I really became aware that what Vera and Tamara had told me the first day was true: the other sick people who were there were only waiting their turns in the gas chamber. I witnessed the people being taken away to the gas chambers.

Every day a truck would come and the people who were so sick that they were not far from death were thrown into the truck. They screamed and struggled, even though they were near death. Even these people - so near death - did not want to die.

We knew where they were going. We felt helpless. But, what could a child do?

Their screams were horrifying. I wonder now if my mother, father and sisters realized what was happening to them. Did they scream? I shall never forget those agonizing screams as those poor people went to the gas chambers.

But, now, after returning to the barracks, my concern was my sister.

CHAPTER 19

I learn how to survive

My happiness at my reunion with Miriam, however, was short-lived. Miriam looked very weak and lifeless. She did not complain nor did she want to talk.

"What is wrong?" I asked her as soon as I returned. "Miriam, what has happened?"

"Nothing," Miriam answered.

"But, there is something wrong," I insisted. "You look so weak, so tired."

"It is nothing, Eva. Leave me alone."

It did not take me very long to realize that Miriam had all the symptoms of being a musselman, that was the camp term for someone who had lost the desire to live. My absence and the toll of the disease had severely affected Miriam.

In 1985 I talked with Miriam and we compared notes. She told me that for the first two weeks when I was in the hospital, she was not taken to the lab and was under SS supervision at all times. She did not know what was going on with me, but she said they were waiting for something to happen. Miriam did not know what, though.

I know today that would I have died, Miriam would have been taken immediately to the lab and killed with a shot to the heart. Then comparative autopsies comparing my diseased organs to Miriam's healthy organs would have been done. Mengele knew that twins are nature's miracle research material, and he used us accordingly.

I didn't die, however; I spoiled his experiments.

Miriam told me that after about two weeks she was taken back to the lab and was injected with some germ that ultimately destroyed her kidneys. It is interesting to note that she was never taken to the hospital. She suffered all her life from kidney problems, and in 1987 her kidneys failed. I donated my left kidney to her because I knew that I had to do something to help my sister, just as I had known in Auschwitz that I had to do something to save her.

However, according to her doctors, the anti-rejection medication that she was given in small doses after the kidney transplant, combined with an unusual substance in her system that the doctors could not identify. The doctors were sure this substance had been in her body since the Auschwitz experiments and caused her to develop cancer of the bladder. Had we been able to find our files, Miriam's life might have been saved. She died of cancer on June 6, 1993.

But, none of that could be foreseen when I returned to the barracks. I only knew that Miriam was very sick. I had to help her.

The next day I volunteered to be a food carrier. It was essential to organize some potatoes from the kitchen for Miriam. I knew camp talk said that was the only food that would work on dysentery. I knew that it would be very difficult for me to do the work I had volunteered for. But, I knew that Miriam was counting on me even though she would not say so.

I really believe that part of the reason she was so weak, so ill was that she thought I was not coming back. I had to help her. I believed we were the only ones left in our family. I could not lose her.

The food carriers had to carry a huge container, very similar to a 30-gallon garbage can, from the kitchen which was located at the end of the row of barracks to their own barracks. Since our barracks was the second one from the front, it would be very difficult to carry that heavy container so far.

Yet, I knew that I had to do it, for only by getting into the kitchen could I organize some potatoes or other food for Miriam.

I was not picked the first day.

The next day I volunteered again, and I was picked to go to the kitchen to get the daily soup.

All the way to the kitchen, my thoughts were "How do I get those potatoes?" When we entered the kitchen, we saw a low, metal table. Next to it was a huge sack, full of potatoes. I knew I had to get some of those potatoes, some how. That was the only way I thought I could save Miriam's life.

I had never stolen anything before in my life, and I had no idea what the camp punishment was for steal-

ing. I only knew that those potatoes held the key to
saving Miriam. I knew that other children were organizing; they had never had to steal before either.
They were succeeding. Surely, I could too. Miriam's
life could be at stake.

When I got near the potatoes, I just bent down. I
could feel three potatoes in my hand. Just then, a big,
fat woman prisoner who worked in the kitchen,
grabbed me and said, "You can not do that."

I innocently replied, "Do what, Madame?"

She looked at me very sternly.

"Child," she said, "it is not nice to steal. Now, put
them back."

I meekly put them back, while silently rejoicing
that I was not going to be more severely punished.
At the same time, I thought to myself, "Here, here in
this place of insanity where they kill mothers in front
of you and where thousands die each day, someone is
telling me that it is not nice to steal." What an irony.
"I guess being a Mengele twin saved me from being
hanged for stealing."

The next day I volunteered again. Because the blocova did not know what I had done - since I did not
get into trouble - I was chosen again.

Now that I knew what I was doing, it was easier to
go into the kitchen, and it was much easier to try to
organize the potatoes without getting caught. I was
not nearly as nervous and because I at least knew
what I was doing this time, I succeeded. I got four
raw potatoes.

It was one of the greatest treasures I had ever had!
I could not wait for evening.

Any clandestine, unauthorized activities, like cooking, had to be done in the evening after the supervi-

sor and the blocova had gone to bed and were supposedly asleep.

Then, someone would use some coal or wood that
had also been organized during the day to bring up a
small fire in one of the ovens at either end of the row
of bricks that ran down the center of the barracks.
Someone would be placed on guard to watch the
door of the blocova to make sure we would not get
caught. We had something like an organized brigade.

I didn't have a pot but I borrowed one from one of
the better organizers, one of the older kids and that
night I boiled the potatoes with the peel and all their
defects. Miriam and I feasted on the four potatoes.
We had no salt or butter, but that did not matter.
They tasted delicious anyway. We ate them peel and
everything, without salt.

Each day after that I volunteered to help carry the
huge container of soup, and I became a very good
organizer. The potatoes that I organized provided
Miriam with enough nourishment that they worked
like a miracle drug on her. She became healthier and
more willing to fight for her own life.

Just as my thoughts of her had kept me alive in the
infirmary, my return to her made it clear to her that
someone cared. It gave her a reason to live. We
would have to fight to survive, but we both knew we
could survive.

Mrs. Csenghery was not in the barracks with us,
but she would sneak in at night. I didn't know at the
time that you were not permitted to leave the barracks at night. She always came at night after curfew.
If she or the other two mothers who sneaked in at
night were caught, I found out later, they were beaten.

In order to cook at night, we organized a guard

system, if you could call it that. Anytime we wanted to cook, we had to wait until the blocova went to sleep. The barracks would be completely dark, as I remember it. Yet, it wasn't totally dark because you could see - like the rats I saw the first night. I did see them; I didn't feel them. You had to be able to find your way to the latrine which was, in our case, at the end of the barracks.

Mrs. Csenghery would sneak in to cook the potatoes for her girls that she had organized. I would cook mine at the same time. We would cook them on some kind of little fire, and there would be five or six pots there. Sometimes after one person would finish, another person would use the pot to cook. But, we always had people on guard to make sure there was nobody coming who would catch us.

We were prepared to do what we had to do to live.

CHAPTER 20

The summer of 1944

Besides being so very ill, I remember something else about the summer of 1944. It was very hot, and there were a lot of bombings. I remember, particularly, being out in the fenced-in area between the two barracks. I was standing beside the wall trying to catch the sun, because that would drive the lice out in the light where we could pick them off.

Suddenly, the sirens would sound. As the sirens were sounding the bombing attack, I watched with delight as the SS soldiers ran to hide. That was the greatest encouragement and sign of hope we had. It was like a game.

A single airplane would come first and would

make a huge, yellow smoke circle over our heads that would encompass the whole camp. We knew that they were not going to bomb inside the circle, only outside. I looked up to the sky, and I saw many airplanes. I knew that they were Americans. I didn't even know that there was a country called the Soviet Union. I couldn't relate to it.

The only good guys I had ever heard about were the Americans. I had an aunt in the United States, but I really didn't have that big an idea what the world was all about and what countries were. Having lived in a small village, I could only relate to what I knew. I didn't know about England or other countries. It was my ray of hope that someday soon we would be free, and the airplanes represented that to me.

When I think about that time, I have a very interesting theory. Let's say that during the whole time we were in camp that summer, there had never been one single plane fly over. I would have had no concept that the outside world was still there. I had no news.

We had no radio. We were cut off, even from the main group of prisoners. We were always under guard because we were guarded very closely Nothing could happen to Mengele's twins. We would hear some camp rumors but we knew a lot less than anybody else in the camp.

How long could a child or any human being live and fight for life without hope? Hope is a very important ingredient in anyone's life and even more important when one must struggle to survive. I believe that if there had been no bombings, no planes, many of the inmates would have died of sheer despair. You have to make a very big effort to live in such situations and without hope, many would not have even tried to continue to survive.

Like many survivors, I wish they had bombed the railroad tracks. That would have been the logical thing to do. If they had only bombed the tracks that led to the camp, the transports would have had to stop for a while. A few people might have been saved. But they didn't do it, and it is a sad thing that they did not.

But, I learned one thing that summer of 1944: you have to struggle to survive. And, hope makes that struggle easier.

CHAPTER 21

The days before Liberation

As the fall of 1944 entered its cold days, I knew that things were changing. In October, there was a huge explosion in one of the crematoria. I was to find out in later years that this was the revolt of the son-derkommando who decided it was better to go down fighting than to go quietly to their deaths. [13] They blew up one of the crematoria in Auschwitz II. It was shortly after that revolt that the Nazi high command ordered that no more Jews were to be gassed at Auschwitz. The gypsy camp was the last camp to be exterminated by the Nazis, and that came in October.

After the gypsies were exterminated, we were moved to their camp. The rumor was that they transferred us because we were going to be gassed. The camp was nearer the crematoria and it was scary to think of being there.

We marched from our camp to that one, and the first day we had to stand for roll call from about 5 a.m. until 4 p.m. It was very cold, and the ground was already frozen. It was already very cold on the eastern plains of Poland, and the air was freezing. My feet froze that day, and so did my sister's. My sister never really recovered from this time outdoors. She always had trouble with her feet.

It was the longest roll call ever. They had to account for every person. Why we were transferred I still do not know, and why it took so long to count us, I do not know either. We lived there in the shadow of the crematoria for about six weeks to two months. Why we were not eliminated, I do not know. We believed they probably had orders for elimination, but maybe we were saved by the orders from Berlin to stop gassing Jews. The SS began to make every effort to eliminate the evidence of the atrocities at Auschwitz.

By late December or early January, there were only three or four barracks with people in them. During the two weeks to a month before liberation, the SS guards had gathered groups of people to leave the camp on forced marches. We heard rumors that the groups of people were marched deep into Germany. A month earlier barracks had been filled to capacity but now it looked like most of the inmates had just disappeared. Most of the people who stayed there were sick or old and could not march.

I remember how the Nazis got people organized to leave when they were preparing to leave the camp.

"Everybody out. Raus, raus. Out, out."

They did go into the barracks and made a small, but not serious, concentrated effort to find people to force out. They did not count the people and try to make sure everyone who could march was ready to march. And, no one ordered us, the children, to join the marches. As a result, we were still in the barracks, and I was determined that I wouldn't go. I figured that we were better off in the barracks because, if we had to, we could run. I said to myself, "I am not going to leave the barrack. I am not going on any march."

So Miriam and I stayed in the barrack and no one came to get us. I was surprised. We found out later there were some twins who went on the march, so apparently we were not all in one barrack. Some of these twins did not get freed until April.

But, we were lucky. Miriam and I did not have to leave the barracks and join the marches.

We had known that something was going on when they began to empty the barracks. In my own mind, I was very clear on what I wanted to do. I did not want to leave the camp or go on any marches. Many of the people, it seemed to me, were willing to go with the Nazis. But not me. I figured very simply that the Nazis weren't very nice to us when they were winning the war, so I certainly didn't want to be near them when they were losing it! They would be a lot worse, I knew. This was a very strange time, for there were no SS, no guards. No one prepared any food for us or worried about us. We saw no guards, no SS.

My time now was spent trying to organize more food so I could try to keep Miriam alive. Food was like medicine to her. We had no medications; food was her only hope.

Now, we were really on our own.

Some of the guys cut the barbed wire so we could go from one camp to the other. We could just walk from area to area, freely. Since we had no food and because I desperately needed shoes, we went to the place where they kept all the clothes - Canada. If you can imagine a place as big as a basketball ball court or a center, huge, filled with piles of clothes, shoes, dresses, blankets - everything, this would be Canada. My sister was not feeling well, so two other girls and I went to search for things. I could not find any shoes that fit, so finally I found a pair of shoes that was huge for the size of my foot, almost twice the size of my foot. I filled the front with some paper I found and I tied them to my feet with string. They at least kept my feet warm.

Miriam's shoes were in better condition because I was the one who was always out walking and looking for something to organize. I remember it was very cold, and we needed warm clothing. We used big blankets to wrap around us to keep us warm.

One afternoon, I went to the kitchen to organize some more bread. In the kitchen, a couple of kids and some grownups were loading up some bread. I heard a strange sound outside. It sounded like some kind of car. I ran to the front door to see what it was and to see what was happening.

There were four SS men outside. Each one had a machine gun.

Suddenly, I noticed that one of the machine guns was pointed at me. The men began spraying bullets everywhere. That is the last thing I remember.

When I awoke later, I felt myself. I wondered if I

were dead. I was sure this was the other world. It took me a long time to realize that I was all right. Thank goodness, my defense mechanisms worked very quickly when I saw the machine guns. I must have fainted or something. Whatever I did, it saved my life. I surely must have fainted the moment I realized what was happening. I remember the head of the barrel being pointed directly at me. The SS probably thought they had killed me. They had no idea who was being killed; they were just spraying bullets in every direction.

It took me some time to get the courage to move my legs. I was sure that I was in the other world when I woke up. I saw bodies around me. Even though I thought I was alive, I wasn't sure.

"Well," I thought, "we are all dead. We are all in the other world. This is how it looks in the other world."

But, then, I moved my legs, and they moved. I tried to move the other person's legs but they would not move. Instantly, I realized that my first thoughts had been right: I was alive, but most of the others were dead.

I got up, and I ran as fast as I could to the barracks. It was quite a distance because the kitchen was at the end of the row of barracks and our barracks was near the front.

"Miriam," I said as I burst into the barracks, "they almost killed me. And, we don't have any bread. I was so scared that I didn't get any."

Then I told Miriam what had happened and how petrified I had been.

"Oh, Eva," she said, "what if you had been killed?"

"I know, I know, what if I had been killed with liberation so close?" We hugged. We were once again survivors. We had each other.

The SS were gone. Apparently the four men had just come back to clear the camp before the liberators arrived.

Suddenly, the same night, we were awakened in the middle of the night by the heat that was coming from the roof. We could feel the heat of the flames through the barracks' walls. We ran outside. The sky was red with flames as far as we could see. The guards had blown up a crematorium and the area known as Canada. Some of the clothes from Canada were even flying through the air as we went out. Everything was red. It looked like the whole world was on fire.

The same four SS lined us up for marching.

"Anyone who doesn't march will be shot!" bellowed one of the guards.

It became a real struggle for life at that point. I knew the best thing to do in this situation was not to be at the end or the beginning or on the outside. For safety, you wanted to be in the middle because you tend to get lost in the crowd and no one pays any attention you. It doesn't matter as much if you walk as fast as everybody else because the crowd will carry you along. It was a struggle, though, to stay in the middle because the group was moving continuously and being pushed by the SS to hurry.

"Miriam, stay with me," I whispered as I moved toward the middle. I held onto her hand very tightly. Together, we worked our way into the middle of the group.

It was only an hour march, but it seemed like an eternity. I don't know how many we lost between

Birkenau and Auschwitz I. They were shooting so many times that we lost count and were very frightened. The bodies fell along the side. I don't know who got killed and who didn't. All of the children and the older people who had not been taken in the earlier marches were in this march. Finally, I recognized the buildings of Auschwitz I. We had been there at least three times a week for months and even though it was the middle of the night, not even daybreak, I recognized it.

As soon as we arrived there, the SS disappeared - almost as if the earth had swallowed them up. We were near a brick building/ barracks, and people were pushing and shoving to get inside, not knowing what was going to happen next. In the shuffle, I lost my sister. I was very scared,and I walked around, crying, calling for her.

"Miriam."

"Miriam, Miriam, where are you?"

Then, I thought to myself, "What if she ends up in another barrack? I might never see her again."

I kept walking around. I was crying and calling Miriam's name. I went from one barrack to another for over twenty-four hours, non-stop, unable to give up my search. Then, miraculously, as I was going into a barrack, I bumped into her. She, too, was crying. I embraced her, and we both cried.

"Eva, where have you been?" she asked me through her tears. And, then, she handed me some chocolate.

We sat down and ate our chocolate. I told her how scared I had been that we would never see each other again.

"Eva, we must not let this happen again," said

Miriam. "We must not get separated."

So, because we thought it would be safer, and we didn't really know where to go, we just decided to stay in the "lucky" barrack where we had been reunited.

I found out later our fears were well-founded. I know of at least two sets of twins who got separated at this moment and were too young to do anything about it. They lost their twin at this moment, so near liberation.

We were here in Auschwitz I about three or four weeks before liberation.

As we got acquainted with our surroundings, we began to organize in order to live. We had been practically on our own for three weeks in Birkenau, and we remained practically on our own until the liberation of the camp. We tried to break into storage places. I always went organizing with two other girls. Miriam would stay in the barracks and watch whatever we had. In addition, she had quite a bit of difficulty walking because her feet had been so badly frostbitten in the roll call I mentioned earlier. Also, she was in poorer health. I tend to run on nervous energy and don't accept failure. It was easier for me to accept the challenge.

We went around to some of the buildings where the SS had lived. We did find some food on a table. We heard rumors that some of it had been poisoned, however, and it wasn't a good idea to eat it. We were afraid to eat it because of those rumors. We did find huge containers of sauerkraut. I mean huge. We ate sauerkraut and drank the juice. We put marmalade on the sauerkraut. There was no water in the faucet and no snow on the ground, so the sauerkraut juice was the only thing we had to drink.

By this time we were very good at making do with things. In one of the basements, we found a huge pile of flour, an enormous pile. I took my scarf — which was our biggest and best tool — straightened it out and filled it up with flour. We mixed it with some liquid and made a cake that we could bake or dry into unleavened bread on top of the stove and then eat.

We had very little food, really. When we did find some bread or something else, we would eat morning, noon and night. I know now that was really very dangerous. In many cases, we were really puffed up, swollen, from eating. If you are on a diet and you start eating everything, you bloat - and we did. Some people died from overeating. One of my close organizing friends did.

One morning the other two twins and I went to the Vistula River which was not far from the camp. We knew there was a river at the edge of the camp, and we needed water. We wanted to break the ice, lower a bottle and fill it up with water. We had a couple of bottles and some small containers in which we could take water back to the camp.

As I was standing on the bank, I saw, on the other side, a little girl who was about my age. She had braided hair, wore a dress and had a coat on. She had a school bag on her back. Obviously, she was going to school.

I froze in place. I could not believe it. I said to myself, "I can't believe it. You mean that there is out there a world where people are clean and where children have braids and nice dresses and go to school?" That was my first revelation that not everybody was in a concentration camp like we were. My whole world for nearly ten months had been the concentration camp, and I could not imagine that somewhere in the world there were children who lived a normal life, had braids with ribbons and were going to school.

I think now, looking back, that thinking everyone was in a concentration camp was part of my defense mechanism. I could think only about the "here and now", struggling to survive was a full time job and a very difficult one. Being so constricted, continuously, not knowing what was going on, day in and day out, only knowing the camp, I could not visualize that any other child or living thing was not in a camp.

I was very upset by this experience. I somehow reasoned that the world had let me down. It was not fair that this child was free and I was not.

We got our water and returned to the camp. The girl had looked at me too. I was wearing ragged clothes, swarming with lice. I don't know what she thought about us.

We went back to the camp and boiled our water so we could kill any contamination. Although we made the trip a couple more times, we did not see the girl again. It was, however, getting quite dangerous to be outside the camp. There was fighting and firing going on all around us. We learned to dodge the barrage from the artillery fire. If it made a certain whining sound, you had to look for cover because the shell was coming in your direction. At that time, the guns were firing indiscriminately and anything or anyone in the way could be hit. We were the battlefield.

During that time, rumors were everywhere that the camp was going to be blown up. Bombs were going off frequently. We could hear the sounds of battle.

There were many indications that the war was drawing very close to us and would soon end.

One day, I remember it being a Saturday, everybody in the barracks was looking out the windows to the right. I could not see anything, but I heard someone shouting, "We are free, we are free!"

"What are you talking about?" I asked.

"Don't you see something coming?" the person asked.

It was snowing, and I was so little that I did not see anything coming. I kept peering through the snow, and finally I saw them - the Soviet Army, wearing all white camouflage outfits, were approaching Auschwitz I. Because of their outfits and the swirling snow, I had not been able to see them until they were up next to the barracks.

We ran out and everybody was hugging and kissing and shouting, "We are free. We are free."

We are free.

We are free.

What magical words. What awesome power they carry.

All I had heard for the past two or three months was that "When we are free we will go home". Now I hoped I could find my mother and father and sisters and go home.

I had survived.

We had beaten the Nazis. We had survived.

CHAPTER 22

Where to now?

Being a child, I didn't think very much about what would happen. I would go home. I took the words "We are free" at their face value.

I went back to our barracks and told Miriam that since we were free, we must get our few belongings together and go home. Everybody was dancing and celebrating, but all I could think of was "I want to go home". Nobody was paying any attention to me, though.

Finally, I went up to someone and asked, "Where do I go?"

"What do you mean?" he asked.

"I mean, where do I go. I'm free, aren't I?"

"Yes, yes," he said, "you are free. But I don't know what to tell you. I guess you can just leave."

As I looked around, I saw others preparing to leave. Some people were walking away from the camp. That brave I wasn't. I realized that I was not so brave that I would just set out. I didn't even know where on the earth I was, much less where my home was. You had to be a little smarter than I, a ten-year-old girl in a concentration camp, to know what direction to start out in and where to go.

The liberation pictures were taken the afternoon of liberation or the following day. There were many people around. They put us in the prisoner uniforms and marched us between the barbed wire. I remember seeing quite a few people with cameras. I was very impressed. My only acquaintance with the movies had been when my mother had taken me to the city to see Shirley Temple in some of her movies.

I remember walking between the barbed wire and thinking, "Why do they want to take pictures of us? Are we movie stars or something?" But, the pictures taken that day have proven to be historic. My twin sister and I were among the first twins to leave. Miriam and I look very chubby. We did have shoes and coats on under the prison uniforms. We were probably heavier than when the SS left because we had eaten everything we could find during the two or three weeks before liberation. There were times when we ate a lot of bread from the kitchen. We also looked chubby because even then we carried everything we had with us — our food, bowls, blankets, everything, because we didn't trust anyone yet. We considered these our treasures, our daily necessities, and we carried them everywhere. Miriam was wearing a dress that hit her above her knees. My dress was longer and warmer because I was the one that had to organize to get enough food for us. I look very chubby in those pictures. My face has always been chubby, no matter what my weight.

I have no idea what I weighed. There were no scales for us to use. I can tell you that just before we left Auschwitz, I remember looking at my sister and thinking, "She looks like a skeleton. I wonder if I look like that too?"

But we were not to leave Auschwitz that day. We stayed there for about two more weeks.

Because we didn't have enough food to eat, I went back to the basement where I had been getting my flour. I filled up my scarf with the flour, and then I heard a shot. Someone began to exclaim, "Nyet! Nyet!"

I was absolutely petrified and thought my freedom - so recently won - was over.

"What is this?" I thought. "I can not go where I want? I can not get food for us to eat?"

I ran out as fast as I could and went back to Miriam. As I ran, I realized the Soviet soldier did not fire at me, like the Germans had. I know now that he was trying to scare me. The Soviets were trying to take control of the camp and get things in order.

I don't remember organizing any more food after that, so maybe we were provided something. I really don't know. The real reason I went to the basement was that we were hungry. It seemed that once we started eating, we were hungry continuously; we just couldn't stop eating. Psychologically, we could not stop even though it was not good for us. So, after that incident, I policed Miriam and she policed me.

We didn't want to die from overeating.

After about four weeks, we were taken by horse and buggy to a monastery in Katowice. At that time, I had a feeling of non-participation because someone else was controlling things. The Soviets worked with the Red Cross and Jewish Refugee Organizations on the liberation and repatriation of camp survivors. They tried to reconnect people or redirect them to wherever they wanted to go. We probably fared better than others.

When we arrived at the monastery, I was unprepared for what I found. There were two beds in a nice, small room - no huge barrack! Beds with clean, white sheets on them. Sheets. Imagine. I was afraid to sit on the beds. I had not seen a white sheet in almost a year and it felt very strange, very out of place. I felt I did not belong to a nice, clean place like that.

I couldn't sleep on the bed either. I felt very uncomfortable because I felt as if I were going to make the sheets dirty. I hadn't slept on sheets or in a bed by myself for about ten months. Everything was foreign to me. I looked at the sheets for a long time. Finally, I pulled them off the bed and went to sleep on the bare mattress.

The first night there, I was very troubled. The nuns had put beautiful toys in our rooms, but I didn't want to play with them. I wasn't in any way impressed or thrilled to find toys to play with. They were just things. The people were not expressing any warmth or love nor did they show they cared for us. That was what I needed. Instead, they thought I was a child who would want to play with toys. But, I had lost my childhood. The innocence I had when I entered the camp, the desire to play with toys, to be a child - these had been lost as I struggled to survive. The toys were an insult to me. I only wanted to go home. I had become obsessed with the idea of going home. After all, I was free, wasn't I? I couldn't understand what the delay was. I have always been impatient and was especially impatient then. Why did it take so long? Why are they stopping us now?

One has to appreciate the situation facing the Soviets. They had found all these miserable souls and were confronted with the problem of trying to figure out what to do with them. The war was still going on and they could not send us home. They asked questions and tried to find out where we wanted to go.

I spoke for us.

"Who are you?" they asked.

"We are twins - that's Miriam, and I am Eva Mozes. Our father is Alexander and our mother is Jaffa. We are from Portz," I told them.

"Where are your parents?"

"I don't know."

"Where do you want to go? Who will take care of you?"

"We want to go home," I kept telling them. "Where else would we go?"

To this, they responded, "Children can not be released if they do not have parents."

"But, we have parents," I protested.

"Where?" they asked.

"I don't know. That is why I must go home to find out if they came back from the camp."

The Soviets considered us to be orphans. Maybe they knew something. Maybe they didn't.

They told us we could not go where we wanted to

unless there was someone to care for us. I could not convince them there would be someone there. We had to stay with them.

I began to wonder: were we really free?

CHAPTER 23

The journey home begins

I felt extremely uncomfortable living in a monastery. It was so very foreign in every single way to me. The Christian praying was difficult for me to handle and their catholic symbols were everywhere. Some of the things that bothered me centered around "What would my father think if he saw me here in this catholic monastery?" I wasn't that religious a child, but what a child learns when he is young does influence that child his whole life. I don't think those who were in charge realized that many of the children had come from very religious families and that the last place they wanted to be after liberation was a religious place not of their choosing. The nuns did not try to convert us, but the place itself made me feel uncomfortable.

We were not prisoners, however. We could leave and go to Katowice. And we did. In the city of Katowice, we could get on any streetcar just by showing our number, and we would ride from one end of the city to another. I am not sure how we learned about this. I know I did not discover it myself. Perhaps the older girls, some of whom were as old as 20, told us.

Riding the streetcar was lots of fun! Just show your number and you could ride. You didn't have to speak Polish, you didn't have to say anything. You didn't have to have money, just get on the streetcar and ride. I have never again done as much riding just for the sheer joy of riding!

We knew that some of the people who had survived Auschwitz were being held in the Displaced Persons (DP) camp at Katowice. Mrs. Csenghery and her twin daughters (who had been selected from our transport and who had been with us in Auschwitz) were there.

One day, I hit upon a plan to get us out of the monastery.

"Come on, Miriam," I said. "We are going to see Mrs. Csenghery."

"But, why?" asked Miriam.

"Never you mind. Just come with me."

And off we went. When we found Mrs. Csenghery, I began talking: "Mrs. Csenghery, you survived with your children. You were my mother's friend. We do not want to stay in the monastery. But, we must because we can not find our parents."

"Yes," said Mrs. Csenghery. "I know. So, why are

you telling me all this?"

I paused, and then I blurted out, "Would you sign a paper saying you are our aunt and get us out so we can go home?"

At first, there was no answer. I am sure she was full of worry about her own family, about her children's health, about her own safety. But, finally, she turned to us and slowly said, "Yes. Yes, I will. I will go to Katowice to the monastery with you and sign the papers. I will take you home with me."

I was so happy. I have never thanked her for what she did, but I will never forget what she did or what it meant to me and Miriam.

That was in March of 1945. We stayed with her until September, 1945, when we joined our real aunt. She always managed to get the best of what was available, I'll tell you that for a fact. If anybody knew how to find the best, Mrs. Csenghery did. She always managed to get a small, separate room for us. Everybody else was staying in huge rooms because the DP camps had been army camps before, so the buildings were really barracks. But, Mrs. Csenghery got a small room for herself, her two daughters, us, and a lady, Mrs. Goldenthal, and her three children. She, too, had been the mother of twins who was selected to go into the camp with her twins. Mrs. Goldenthal is in the liberation pictures, too, carrying her little girl. At the time, I did not think to ask her how she managed to save her little girl, but I found out later when I was in Israel that Mrs. Goldenthal was religiously dressed which meant she was wearing a very long skirt. As she looked around on the ramp, she was trying to make some sense of what was happening when the transports unloaded. She saw children being taken on the left, and so she hid her little girl under her long skirt. The little girl, now grown, remembers only one thing about that time — unusual darkness. As they waited, when the little girl would ask to come out, her mother would reply, "Just a little bit longer, please." She hid her under her skirt and took her with her to the barracks. She kept her in the barracks; they would hide her under the mattress when inspection was held.

Mrs. Goldenthal and Mrs. Csenghery cleaned us, washed us and boiled our clothes. They got rid of all our lice. They fixed special food for us. We were under the supervision of the Soviet army and got bread from them. They also gave us half a ruble every week to spend on something we wanted.

In addition to the liberated prisoners of Auschwitz, the refugee camp had Italian prisoners of war in it. We cut the barbed wire so we could go back and forth between the camps more easily and traded with them. We had only to show our numbers to the Russian guards to leave the camp, so we would go to the open air market in Katowice to buy items and trade them. There was not a great deal at the market because the war was still going on. People were still trying, however, to sell any extra items they had. We would buy an apple or a fruit. It was an interesting experience to see how some of the villagers in the Soviet Union lived. The heavy fighting had left its mark though because there were ruins everywhere.

The DP camp was interesting. The Italian soldiers in the camp were always singing and were always trying to reach the women in the second story of our building. I assume it was an army barracks because it could house people, and it had lots of army cots in it.

They were not allowed to come into our building, so I particularly remember one day when they climbed onto a scaffolding and used the ropes to haul themselves up to a second-floor where the women were. I looked out the window, and I saw somebody going up. It was the Italian prisoners going up to court the women! They sang serenades to them. They also put on big shows in the open air theater on the stage. They would sing and do all kinds of funny things. They would make stage curtains out of blankets which they would pull together and then open for the show. It was a big thing to go to the show. I was very impressed with their ingenuity to make the stage, the curtains and the show out of nothing.

After about a month and a half, I was awakened from a very deep sleep by Mrs. Csenghery who told us to pack everything because we were moving. We got everything together, and our small group, along with the others, was put on a train.

I once again heard the clickety-clack of a train.

Where would we go this time?

I wondered.

CHAPTER 24

Free, but not free

Again, we entered a cattle car. But, it had two rows of bunks on each side of the car, away from the doors; it was empty in the middle. The bunks were as wide as the car and deep enough to sleep four people easily. You could sit there and watch the mountains and scenery. We loved to sit on the top bunk bed and look out the windows which were not covered by barbed-wire. My only problem was that I had extreme pain in my side whenever I moved. I do not know what it was or what caused it, but my joy of traveling as a free human being was dampened by the sharp pain in my side.

The train seemed to be going at a very slow pace.

As we traveled, they all talked about what they were going to do when they got home. During this time, Mrs. Csenghery kept saying over and over, "I'll tell my story. I'll tell my story. I will tell them what these monsters did to us." What was going on with me seemed to remind her of what she had witnessed and experienced. I couldn't imagine then who would want to hear about Auschwitz. To me, in my own mind, I did not understand for a very long time that not all the world, not all the people in the world had ever heard of concentration camps or understood or knew what went on in them. Everybody I knew at that point had been in a concentration camp, and I just couldn't comprehend that people had not been sent to such places. I knew that those people who were on the train with us did not want to hear about Auschwitz, yet Mrs. Csenghery kept talking about it, saying she was going to look for the guilty ones and was going to get justice. She kept talking about it.

All I wanted was to find my parents or somebody from my family.

We went from Katowice to Czernowitz which was very close to the Rumanian border in Czechoslovakia, only about 30 km. We thought we were getting closer to home and were going to get to go home soon. But, we didn't. We stayed in Czernowitz about two months and then went to another DP camp.

The Czernowitz camp was very similar to the other camp; it was on the outer edge of the city. We could go into town to the open air market and buy something we wanted. We would walk through the village and no one bothered us. There were a lot of bombed-out houses. The camp could have once been an army camp or labor camp or even a ghetto.

I loved to go outside the camp and explore the surroundings. One day I came upon an unusual U-
shaped hill. It was a perfect U. It was covered with
lots of beautiful wild flowers.

The top of the hill was about 15 to 20 feet high and
had the most colorful bright red flowers on it. So I
huffed and puffed because the hill was steep and I
finally reached the top.

I picked a beautiful bouquet of the red flowers to
take Mrs. Csenghery to thank her for taking care of
us. On my climb up I had bumped into some big
chunks of bones, and I was confused by them. I did
not understand what they were doing there.

I cheerfully ran to our little room to give the flowers to Mrs. Csenghery. She thanked me and asked
me, "Where did you find them?"

"On top of that U-shaped hill and I climbed to the
top to get them - for you," I answered.

Immediately, Mrs. Csenghery scolded me.

"Don't you ever go there again. Don't you know
hundreds and thousands of Jews were buried there
alive because the Nazis ran out of ammunition and
those hills moved up and down for three days until
they all died!?!"

I was stunned.

"I am so sorry. I didn't know about it. I will not
trample on those graves again."

I realized that day that besides Auschwitz, Jews
were murdered, even in the Nazi-occupied Soviet
Union. [15]

Then, once again, we were told to pack up. We
were moving again. We were loaded onto the cattle
cars with the bunk beds in them. They were fairly
nice and comfortable, compared to those other cattle

cars we had ridden in so long ago. We knew that it wasn't the same kind of cattle car in which we had gone to Auschwitz, and we knew from our first trip that we were really only changing camps.

It was late spring. Flowers were blooming, birds were chirping. We were singing - "It is good to be alive!"

As our train went deeper into Soviet territory, the people became a bit frightened and troubled. I didn't understand their feelings. Many times, as the train was moving very slowly on a bed which went up hill, people would jump off and roll down the hill into the woods away from the train. I wondered "Where are they going?" "Why are they jumping off?" "What is their problem?" I did not understand that many people, even after months in a concentration camp, knew enough about communism to know they did not want to live under communism. I often wondered what happened to them.

Just going deep into the Soviet Union didn't seem to be a problem to me then, but I can see now where the people who knew about it were frightened. At times, the train would stop and would stay for half a day, and Mrs. Csenghery would take two bricks, make a little fire and stir up some food. We would get enough bread and rations from the Russians that we were not starving, but we were never overfed. After about a week, we arrived in another camp, Slutz. It was very close to Minsk in Byelorussia. We stayed there until September.

Finally, in September, people were grouped by the country of their origin: Greek, Hungarian, Rumanian, French, Dutch. Actually, the people on the train whom the Russians had liberated were from all over

Europe. We were grouped and housed according to the country of origin from then on. Suddenly, one day, in late September, I don't know why, we started back into Rumania. The first place we stayed was Nagy Várad, which was the place of origin of Mrs. Goldenthal, her twins - Alex and Ernö" - and her daughter Margarita. One of the children is still there; the other two are in Israel. She died in 1982.

A Jewish agency gave us some money to stay in a hotel and to eat. I remember how very, very good the food was. Nagy Várad was to the north of Portz, our village, and it was on a major thoroughfare of railroad tracks. We arrived in Simleul Silvanei the next day. A worker told us that our aunt was inquiring about us, talking to the agency. Every little town that had had a Jewish population now had a Jewish Agency to help reunite families and help displaced persons. Mrs. Csenghery kept us overnight. The next morning a cousin of ours showed up and he took us on the train to return home.

September, 1945. We were going home.

CHAPTER 25

The return to Portz

Within a short time, we had arrived at Portz. We
got off the train at the top of the hill and walked
through the village to our home. As I approached the
house, my heart was beating so hard that I could hear
the beats. Finally, after this horrible nightmare, I was
home again. My memories of the house and what
was there were of the good things and good times,
and I could see none of that was left. The weeds were
very tall. Everything looked very neglected. It was
all very abandoned, very empty. It was extremely
painful and very disappointing. After I saw the
house, I very quickly realized that my father and
mother had not returned. They would never have let

the weeds grow up so high. They would never have let the house run down so much.

I suddenly realized that Miriam and I were all that was left of the Mozes family. There was nobody else. No mother. No father. No Edit. No Aliz.

But, surprise, surprise. Suddenly, my mother's old dog, Lilly, a red dachshund, was standing before us, wagging her tail. I guess Jewish dogs were not taken to concentration camps.

We entered the house.

It was all so desolate, both inside and outside. The house had been ransacked and not much had been left behind. The house was empty, and so was my heart. As I walked from room to room to try to find any reminders, any remnants of the life I had once lived, I found one badly crumpled picture. The picture I have of the family was the last picture taken of us, and I found it all wadded up on the floor. I picked it up and saved it. It was the only proof I had that once, not so very long ago, I had a family.

My cousin was staying there and working the land. He had fixed up one of the rooms. He had, at that time, one bed, one table, and a couple of chairs - all of which he had recovered from neighbors who had looted our house after we were taken away. It seemed as if everybody in the village had something from our house. At one point, I visited the lady across the street who had been friends with my mother. I wanted to know if she had seen my mother. When I entered her house, I saw some of the linens from my sisters' dowries on her table.

"Why do you have those?" I asked her.

"Oh, I just took them to save them for you and your sisters," she said. "Here, I will return them to you."

"No," I said. "I don't want them."

I was very hurt that she, too, must have participated in the looting of our house.

My cousin had set up headquarters in the summer kitchen.

"No, I have not seen anyone from your family," he answered to our questions about Mother and Father. "I know only that your Aunt Irén survived and is waiting for you."

Although our aunt had been sent to a concentration camp, she had survived. We were among the last to return. For some reason, we had been taken so deep into the Soviet Union that we were among the last of the Jews to be returned. Our aunt had returned in May when the war was over. We did not return to Rumania until September. My aunt had found out about us from checking the lists of survivors that were coming in from the Red Cross. We found out later she had known exactly when our transport was to arrive in Portz. From the time she had arrived home, she had checked daily to see if anyone from our family had survived.

Aunt Irén was among the very few aunts that we knew very well. She would visit us once a month in her chauffeur driven car with her son, Laci, who was a young, handsome attorney. He would always play games with us and let us win. She was the youngest girl in my father's family and was very close to my father.

I really did not feel very comfortable there even though it was our house. No one from our family was there. There was really no place to stay, and I didn't want to stay with our cousin. I didn't feel like I belonged there any more. The next day our cousin

took us by horse and buggy to the city to join our
aunt. Our cousin provided us with some food
because he told us food was very scarce.

We had no home, no family.

We were alive.

We were free.

We were alone.

CHAPTER 26

Struggling to adjust

At first, we were very happy to be with our aunt. We had always liked to visit her. She was more than willing to take us in, but we did become, in time, a big problem. It was an unwritten agreement after the war because there were so many orphaned children that the relative who took those children in became their surrogate mother. Her new husband became our surrogate father.

It was a very patched-up family. My aunt's husband had died in the concentration camps. She said then she did not know about her son. She married a man who had lost his wife and daughter in the camps. Since they were married only in the syna-

gogue, the Rumanian government did not recognize
their marriage. They would have had to get married
in a civil ceremony for the state to recognize the marriage. My aunt was opposed to this for several reasons, so we became a family with three last names.
We didn't know, and never really learned, how to be
a family. Each one of us was still mourning the death
of our own family. We all needed love and caring
and no one was capable of giving us that at that time.

We did have some good times, but there were some
bad times too. My aunt, like her brother, my father,
did not discuss any of her problems with us. I felt
she was more concerned with herself than she was
with us. If we had any problems, she was not very
understanding. I do not ever remember her giving us
a hug or a kiss or a kind word. And, we needed to be
hugged and kissed so much. She would go to work
and somehow seemed always to be busy doing something. We yearned for a bit of caring; she was very
cold. I know she cared; she was the only one willing
to take us in and the only one who looked out for us.
I know now she probably was trying to overcome her
own personal problems because of what she had been
through during the war. But, so were we, and we
were children, and we needed more than a figure
head in our lives. I am sure I was a very difficult
child. Miriam was always milder nor did she have as
sharp a tongue.

We had another aunt and two cousins who were in
Bucharest during the Holocaust and were never
deported. This was my Aunt Ferike Néni. Her husband owned a factory before the war and had been
allowed to continue to run it. It made some kind of
essential material, like cars. My two cousins were

about my Aunt Irén's age because Ferike Néni was one of the oldest of my father's brothers and sisters and Irén was the youngest. Aunt Ferike Néni never seemed to want to be bothered with us. All she would do was maybe once a month invite us for an ice cream or take us out to the movie. She would give us chocolate to take home. That was about it. She was pleasant but very cold.

For some reasons, in those days, I liked her better, even though I knew that my Aunt Irén had asked her to take us in and she had refused. My Aunt Irén had explained to her that she (Ferike) had a nice home, her children were grown and she would be able to provide for us, her brother's children, better. But Aunt Ferike told my aunt that she was too busy, she traveled a lot. So my Aunt Irén kept us.

If Aunt Irén had not taken us in, I suppose, like others, we would have spent most of our teenage years in an orphanage. We had it better than those who went from camp to camp or were sent to orphanages. It was not easy for her, however, because we had nightmares for at least five years after the war, up until the time we went to Israel, and we also had many health and emotional problems.

Because a friend of hers was the principal of the gymnasium Queen Mary, we were soon enrolled in school even though our Rumanian was not as good as our Hungarian. We began school soon after our arrival, wearing the Russian tunics we had been given by the Russians who had guarded us so long.

We were fortunate, in some ways, because we had been allowed to attend school until the time we were deported, unlike many Jews. We had really missed only one and a half years of school, and since we had the fraulein in our home who tutored our older sisters, we were not very far behind in our studies.

Life continued for us, but not without problems. Even then, I wanted to grow up like a normal child, having a mother, father, sister, relatives. I didn't want to have nightmares about rats as huge as cats or dead bodies or having needles injected into me. I would often get angry and become frustrated. Yet, we continued.

In 1946, not too long after we began living with my aunt, the first of many medical problems we would have as a result of being at Auschwitz began to develop. We were suffering from malnutrition, and our systems were so weakened that we began to get every disease you could think of - particularly colds and allergic reactions. We both began to develop pimples on our arms that turned into huge scars about two inches in diameter all over our arms and legs. They were awful, very painful. So, our aunt took us to the doctor.

Knowing some of what we had been through at Auschwitz, our aunt tried to reassure us when we got to the doctor's office.

"Children, he will not hurt you," she told us as we approached the office. But I was not so sure; I had learned not to trust doctors. I was never comfortable in a doctor's office, but always acted like a little soldier - if it had to be done, it had to be done.

Once inside, just like at the camp, we had to undress. I became even more uncertain. Our aunt was allowed to stay with us.

A doctor in a white coat came in and began examining us.

"Say ah-h-h," he said, sticking a tongue depressor

into each of our mouths. Then he proceeded to check our glands and listen to our lungs. Finally, he examined the sores and the scars forming from them.

"Well, doctor, what is it?" my aunt asked.

"These children have what many war children are suffering from. Their bodies are showing the ill effects of malnutrition. There is nothing wrong with them that vitamins and a good diet can not fix. But, in this time, who can provide either?"

Certainly, my aunt tried. She tried to get us vitamins, but they were not available. She stood in line and had us stand in line for bread, but after five or six hours we would reach the front of the line only to be told there was no bread. There just simply were no commodities available for the public. As a result, we frequently ate at a near-by orphanage. My aunt hired our cousin to run the farm and to grow food for us on my father's farm.

Our cousin sent us flour, potatoes, sunflower oil, wheat, fruits, vegetables and eggs. Whenever the food would arrive, I would drink the oil right out of the bottle. My aunt was scared it would hurt us. She had been in the camps too, but she had worked in a factory and being an adult, the deprivation had not affected her like it had affected us.

It was because of this strange eating problem that our aunt took us back to the doctor.

"Doctor," she said when she took us back, "these girls are drinking oil right out of the bottle. I do not know what is wrong with them. I am afraid it will hurt them."

Carefully, the doctor examined us again. Finally, he turned to my aunt and said, "Let them eat whatever they can. Obviously the sunflower oil must have some vitamins and minerals they need. They are not getting sick from it. If anything, they are better."

The food sent by our cousin also caused us to get into trouble one day. My aunt owned a big apartment house. The state had let her have it since she was a war widow and a survivor of the camps. We lived in an elegant first floor apartment with a small veranda overlooking the court yard.

One day, I was eating some white bread on the little veranda and someone saw me and reported me to the secret police. That evening the secret police came and asked us where the white bread was. Since we made our own bread from the flour our cousin sent, we told them we had no bread.

In a search of the apartment, however, they found the flour and confiscated all the food we had from the farm. They told us we were "sabotaging the system" and we could not have anything but what our rations allowed.

The next day, my aunt built a fake cabinet that looked like a wall. You could get in there only by pushing a button. From then on, we hid our flour and the food we got from the farm there. She warned us not ever to open the door if she was not home.

We were beginning to find out that freedom was not what we had thought it would be.

We were beginning to realize the beautiful words the new communist system chanted were just empty slogans.

We had exchanged one oppressive system for another.

CHAPTER 27

Life begins again in Rumania

Life was not easy for us. We had no decent clothes when we returned, only the tunics given to us by the Russians. My aunt didn't have anything to speak of either. There were no stores where you could buy anything. Luckily, my aunt in the United States mailed us packages, and one package included some material so my Aunt Irén could make us dresses. That's how we got our first two dresses after the war.

All the children always made fun of us because of our clothes. We didn't speak good Rumanian and even then anti-Semitism was still alive. In fact, it was rampant. They called us "Dirty Jews" even after what we had been through. We were the only two

Jews in the high school where my aunt enrolled us. There was another high school later, all Jewish, and I met two of the students there once. They were very religious and I had no interest in any kind of religious school.

Actually, there were not too many Jews, just a handful, some of whom had survived concentration camp and others who had survived by escaping to Switzerland. There were two sets of twins in Cluj - Lea and Menoshe Lorenczy whose father survived and Judit Rosenbaum whose sister died but her mother survived. We envied them.

In 1946, there was even a rumor in Cluj that there was a Jewish vampire going around stalking people and sucking their blood as they were walking the street and this caused me problems. It seems at this time that we were always hungry, even though we had a little food coming in from the farm. After school, we would go to an orphanage to eat the evening meal and would walk home in the dark. I was worried because we were walking home late at night and I was afraid that the vampire wouldn't know I was Jewish and would attack me. You have to be a twelve-year-old child to understand that even though these were just rumors, I believed them. My biggest worry was how I would tell the vampire I was Jewish if he attacked me. I never questioned who came up with the idea or why such rumors were being spread about Jews, so I understand how easy it is to spread false and dreadful rumors.

Rumania had become communist in 1947, but, actually, the communist party was ruling Rumania right after the Germans fell back. The Republic was proclaimed in 1947. Right after liberation, you could tell a lot of things were going on in the communist party. I became involved in the party.

As a child who had come back from the camps, I was intrigued with the talk of freedom, brotherhood and liberty. I became a member of the communist youth party. Since we had been very, very wealthy people, we would have been subjected to very severe punishment, even jail, because anybody who had any land or factory was jailed for exploiting the poor. But, as war orphans, they were willing to ignore our background. Besides, I heard a lot of talk about "surviving" and I knew in some way I must have accomplished something. We were not subjected to any kind of persecution by the communists or the government of Rumania, just the people who had not let their anti-Semitism die. The party welcomed me because I was a camp survivor and treated me so royally that I thought, "Gosh, all of a sudden, I am a big shot!" I also believed that now they wouldn't call me a "Dirty Jew" anymore. I was important.

As I became involved in the communist party in the high school, it seemed to be like a boys' club or girls' club, not like anything evil. It became the "in" thing to be a member. Nobody really knew what it was. We went to meetings, studied about Marxism and Leninism, participated in parades, marches, picnics, saw movies and felt like a part of something.

The schools were completely governed by the communist party; if they didn't want somebody to get an education, they simply saw to it that he couldn't get into school. For instance, anybody who came from an aristocratic family before was not permitted to go to high school. Children of farmers, laborers or the proletariat had first choice. There were only as many schools as they permitted.

I became involved in the communist party just because of sheer enthusiasm and because it sounded like something good. I was very flattered when they appointed me head of the selection committee. I had not accomplished anything up to that time to prove that I would be a good committee chairman. But, I loved the honor after the concentration camp. I know now it was a plan to trap us, but I did not understand that then. They wanted to make the disenfranchised feel important and, therefore, make them feel grateful and be loyal communists.

I became the leader of the girls. My aunt kept saying to us, "You are getting too deeply involved; it is not good, it is not good."

"But, Aunt," I said, "what harm can there be? "

"You'll get into trouble, you shouldn't listen to them."

I didn't know then what she was talking about. I believed the talk about freedom, brotherhood and equality. How could I get into trouble? I had never had anyone tell me about communism or what it meant. At the age of twelve, you can not make sense of something if you haven't heard about it.

Looking back, I admit there were some things I couldn't quite buy. We were taught in school that the United States was imperialistic. I thought, "Gosh, I am getting all these packages from there, so how can it be the people are so terrible and have all these wonderful things?"

They couldn't quite shove all this down my throat, but they were trying to brainwash us from morning to night. They succeeded with some of the kids, I am sure.

It was not until 1948 that I really saw what communism was all about. I got into trouble with the party. Up until then, I went along with the party idea of only the best kids being in the party, and they had to be the best students and set examples. It was not a question that they asked this of us - they demanded it. If the kids did not meet their standards, they got kicked out of the party and without the party, there was no school.

In May of 1948, a major parade - the May Day parade - was planned. I was the leader of thirty kids and my sister was also a leader. Our groups were the pioneers and we wore red neck ties. We were supposed to march in the morning at a parade. At noon we were going to have a picnic in the park near a forest and at night we were supposed to participate in a torchlight parade.

We marched in the parade and we went to the picnic. But, there was a long time between the picnic and the torchlight parade. I knew the party expected the students to be the best in their classes, so I decided that it was a lot more important for the members of the group to go home to study since the students had a test the next day rather than to wait around for a torchlight parade. In Europe students go to school six days a week, so Sunday is their only day off or holy day. I thought they needed the time. So, I sent them home. It was a very simple and very innocent act.

It was no big deal to me. I did not ask for permission. It made good sense to me to send the girls home; I was the leader. It did not occur to me that I would have to go ask for permission. I made what I thought was a logical decision.

The next day I was called to the headquarters. I remember that day well. I will never forget it.

The headquarters was a big theater with a promenade area. If you wanted to see your boyfriend or anybody else, you would go there because everybody would gather there and walk and talk. The offices of the Youth Communist Party were upstairs in this building.

When I arrived, the chairman of the Youth Communist Party was waiting. I had worked with him many times as a volunteer selling tickets for some gymnastic events, conferences, gatherings, festivals and dancing.

I went in and sat down.

"Where were you yesterday?" he asked angrily.

"Well, the kids have to be good students because I understand the communists have to be the best, and they had been there all day long, they had gone to the parade and the picnic, so I thought..."

He rudely interrupted me, "You thought?"

"Yes, sir."

"You are not supposed to think. You are supposed to follow orders."

Suddenly, thoughts of Auschwitz came rushing over me. I did not say anything out loud, but I was wondering what they were going to do to me that had not already been tried.

"Yes," I said. "I think. And if I can not think, I do not want to be in your party. I'll get out of the party."

He laughed. He paused. Then, he said, "You are the most stubborn person I have ever met. You can not get out of this party. We can kick you out, but that means you can not attend school in this country ever. Clear?"

Now, I was beginning to get a little bit scared. Here I was, 13-years-old and my life was already over? Just because I had "thought"? Where was I going to go? I wasn't going to be able to finish school, and at that time I had wanted to study medicine. I had learned Rumanian very quickly, and it had been clear from the beginning that I was an excellent student. I was working very hard to get good grades so I could go to medical school.

I looked at him, and I said, "Well, I guess that I will just have to do what you are telling me, then."

But, I didn't mean what I said.

CHAPTER 28

Israel - a dream becomes reality

Shortly after my trouble with the party, Israel became a country. I began to think it would be an extreme privilege to live in a place where my father had dreamed of living. I remembered that the last time we had seen our father, he had made us promise that if we survived, we would go to Israel. I became excited about the thought of a place like Jerusalem and living in a Jewish country.

I had always thought that many of the stories my father had told us were fairy tales. Yet, I also remembered that was really the only time I enjoyed listening to him. His dreams of Israel had been real. Now they became my dreams.

The man my aunt had married after the war was a pharmacist. I did not know that the profits from his business went to the communist government. In 1948, one night, the police came, knocked on the door, and he was taken away. We had no idea where he was or what was happening to him. My aunt told us not to answer the door again - even if the police did come.

Then, one night, my aunt came to us. She took us into a room, and she said, "Children, I want you to know. I am very excited. My son is alive, and he is living in Israel."

We were excited too. Her son had been our favorite cousin, and it was exciting to think he could still be alive.

Letters began coming from Israel, and finally my aunt said we should go to Israel because she would like to live with her son. We applied for visas. My aunt's exit visa was granted very easily. It took us two years to get ours, however, because every government wants to keep its young people. Nobody wants the old people.

My aunt also applied for a visa in the name of the man she had married; his name was Alexander Hirsch.

We began to prepare to leave Rumania. The rules were changing daily about what we could take. We packed one year before we left and for one year we lived surrounded by those boxes filled with the things we hoped to take with us. We were going to take whatever we had, but that was not much - three or four dresses, a coat. We had to sign all kinds of papers. I am assuming that in order to leave, everything we owned had to be signed over to the

Rumanian government, including our two dunam (acres) of land and our home in Portz. The rest of the farm was confiscated by the Rumanian government in 1947.

About two months before we were to leave, my uncle was released from prison and given a visa to leave the country, as well. He wouldn't say a word about what had happened to him. In fact, he did not talk after being released from prison. We didn't press because we were just so glad he had been released.

Finally, in June, when we were about to leave, the government told us that all we could take with us was what we could wear. The day we left for the ship, my aunt made us wear three dresses and our coats. I was smart enough to figure out that she wanted us to have some clothes when we got to Israel.

Our ship was the next to last ship to leave. After the next ship, exit visas were stopped altogether.

When we got on the ship, my uncle broke his long silence.

"First of all, I am a fool. I have lived a lie. I hope you will remember this. I worked for the Rumanian underground and was imprisoned during King Michael's reign. After concentration camp, I worked hard and all the money I earned went to the communists. I was getting a salary. When I saw what they did with their power, I started speaking out against communism. It was a mockery of liberty and freedom."

He continued, "When I saw what they did with their power and how they were only out for themselves, I realized they were only looking out for their own. We were not important to them anymore. I wasn't going to stand for it any more so to quiet me down, they put me in a labor camp. I was sent there without a trial just to shut me up, and they did. It was a mockery of the things I had suffered for."

"Then, what are you doing here?" I asked.

"They let me out because I said I was going to Israel."

"I think now, looking back, that anyone who is a communist must be one by the time he is 16 and he must not have a heart because the ideals - equality, brotherhood, liberty - are beautiful. But, if that same person is still a communist at 26, I believe he doesn't have a brain. It just doesn't work; it is all phony," he said.

When we arrived in Israel, we had a surprise waiting. My cousin was not in Israel. He did die in the camps. My aunt had made up the whole story to get a visa and not arouse the suspicion of the Rumanian government. The letters were written by a cousin in Israel, my uncle's son-in-law. I was shattered when I found this out because I had loved this cousin so. I also could not understand that the world was so confining that one had to make up stories to get his freedom. Even today, when I meet someone who leans toward the left, I always tell him, "Go, try it out. If you like it so well - if you like for everybody to tell you how to breathe, what to wear, when to go to bed - then maybe that is the right place for you."

Believe me, Freedom is the most precious gift we have.

CHAPTER 29

Life begins in Israel

When we arrived in Israel, we did not really arrive
as a family. My aunt had her family name, my uncle
his, and we were still bearing the name of Mozes. My
uncle Aaron (father's brother) who had gone to Israel
in 1935 met us at the port. We had mailed him a picture in 1948, and he had resolved that we were going
to get all the help he could give us and that he would
try to ease our suffering. He made such promises to
us that we thought we would just eat chocolate and
oranges in Israel and be happy.

We disembarked in Haifa. The way Haifa is built,
Mt. Carmel is in the background. As our ship
docked, the sun was just creeping over the mountain

and everybody burst into the Israel national anthem. People were crying, singing and dancing with joy.

The trip there is a story in itself. It was somewhat a mixed blessing. I never saw a cabin on the trip. I never even knew at that time that ships had cabins. That ship was built for 300 people and there were 3,000 people on it. It was the last ship that left for Israel for two years because for the following two years, all visas to Israel were stopped.

We had to stand in line, pushing and shoving to get our visa to get on the ship and then we waited for twenty-four hours on board before we set sail.

I was exhausted by the time we got on the ship. I was wearing three dresses and a top coat. It was a long, tiring trip even once we got started. It was very exciting to be on the open sea, watching the dolphins jump in and out of the ocean. All we could see was water and more water. No land was in sight for days and days. We watched the sailors get the ship ready for a storm that never came. This was all very new and intriguing for me.

When we got off, my uncle hugged us and kissed us. We got to spend the afternoon with him. We met my cousin and her children for the first time. As newcomers, however, we were not allowed to stay with my uncle yet. That evening we were taken to the headquarters for immigration. Every immigrant who entered the country had to be under quarantine for a period of time. It was only because my uncle worked in the port that we were allowed to go with him that afternoon. My uncle transported immigrants from the port to the immigration center, and he had actually sneaked us out for the day. It was against the rules, but he wanted to see us and have us meet the rest of the family.

We were all sent to absorption centers. My aunt and uncle went to one, Miriam and I to another. We were sent to a children's village somewhere in Israel for the initial six weeks in quarantine. We were given all kinds of immunization shots and Israeli clothes, including shorts, which were new to us.

Immediately we were processed; we were showered, interviewed and had our photographs taken. We actually looked fairly good.

We were glad that we did not have to stay with my aunt but could be with the children. I think that we were really tired of her pushing us around. I said to myself that day, "Now, I don't need you any more, Aunt Irén. I know that you have taken care of us and that is nice, but you never give us any love, and I don't need you any more."

I know she cared, but there was no love in her caring. This was what I missed the most. We were hungry for affection, and she did not provide any affection.

We were sent to a huge agricultural farm village where you work half a day and go to school half a day. These agricultural farms were supported by the Hadassah organization, a women's Jewish organization in the U.S.A., and by the Israeli government. The Youth Aliyah Villages were actually begun in 1934 to save children from the Holocaust. Now, in 1950, the children who were not saved from the Holocaust were coming to inhabit them.

We were in that village with about 300 or 400 other children, and there were about 100 villages. It is a big program. There are hundreds of thousands of graduates of these Youth Aliyah Villages.

The village was organized so that anybody entering it was immediately made to feel welcome. The first day we went into a little reception room. There were two boys from Iraq who came at the same time. Not all of the children in the villages were survivors of the Holocaust, and not all of them were orphans. Some of them had parents but their economic situation as refugees made it impossible for them to provide for their children. Sometimes, the children and parents were separated, and the children placed in the village while the parents went to learn a trade or to learn the language and get settled in. The children could learn the language and receive an education and training at the Aliyah while their parents were being trained.

I fell in love with one of the two boys from Batzra, Iraq. I had an awful crush on him. He already spoke Hebrew. I admired him because he was a gorgeous young man. He knew a lot about living in Israel, which I didn't. To learn the language faster, I took a pen and paper and would ask him what something was and he would write it down in Hebrew. Within three months I spoke Hebrew fairly well. By the time I had left Rumania, I had spoken Rumanian very well, especially considering the first year in school I had almost failed because I did not know the language well enough to understand what they were teaching. Learning a new language was not that great an accomplishment for me by then, but it was important and a challenge and I took it to heart.

On the farm, I worked picking tomatoes, picking peanuts, and I was in a special group of milk maids. I don't know why, but I have always tried to figure out what was the best thing to do and what was the best thing to learn. I heard that being a milk maid was special and I got to be a milk maid and got special privileges. I was the only girl who worked in there with all the guys, and I sure liked that! I wanted to be around young men.

The first night we were there was Friday night, the Shabbot. After working in the fields, we came back and cleaned up and that night 300 kids, all dressed in white gathered in a huge dining room and welcomed the Shabbot, saying the prayers and singing and dancing to lots of songs.

A girl was assigned to me as a sort of big sister, and one was assigned to my sister. We immediately were made to feel welcome and joined in the dances and songs. The camps had been set up by psychologists and they were organized to make the new comer feel accepted into the group, regardless of age.

For the first time since I had left the camp, I slept without having any nightmares. It was a feeling of freedom I probably will never have again.

I wish I could have two more years like that.

During that time, I got up without having to worry about anyone calling me a "Dirty Jew"; I didn't have to worry about my aunt pestering me or criticizing me or being nagged at about helping.

We had to take care of our own rooms. We used to sleep under the beds in the summer because the floors were tile and were much cooler; we often took naps under the beds to escape the summer heat. We would get up very early when the sun was not very hot and would work until noon, then take a nap during the heat of the day. After our naps, we would go back to work.

We stayed there two years. I think that anybody who has problems should be allowed to spend time in a Youth Aliyah village/school. For me, it was a place where my hurts, my pains, my sufferings were able to begin to heal.

At the end of the two years, in 1952, I enlisted in the Israeli Army.

Life was to go on - but the echoes from Auschwitz would haunt me and influence me for the rest of my life.

NOTES

1. Film of the liberation, available at the Auschwitz State Museum, Auschwitz, Poland.

2. This figure comes from *War Against the Jews* by Lucy Dawidowicz, pg. 382.

3. This figure comes from *Atlas of the Holocaust* by Martin Gilbert, pg. 196, map 254.

4. According to research by Mel Mermelstein in *By Bread Alone*, this pattern of delay was part of a massive fund raising. In Budapest three Jewish committees were set up to ransom the Jews and raised about 1.6 million dollars - only to get 600 Jews released for Palestine. In this same time period, according to Mermelstein, Adolf Eichmann demanded two hundred tons of coffee, two hundred tons of tea, two thousand cases of soap and ten thousand trucks in his demand to turn off the gas at Auschwitz-Birkenau, pp. 85 - 91.

5. Most survivors tell of being allowed to take only their personal belongings with them with a limit of about 60 pounds per person being placed on baggage.

6. The ghetto from which Eva Mozes Kor and her family left was at Szilagysomlyo and contained 7,000 people. According to Martin Gilbert, *Atlas of the Holocaust,* they were shipped out on May 3, 1944.

7. The absorptive capacity of the camp was determined by the number of people who could be killed at one time. That meant approximately 4,000 people could be sent to the gas chambers at any one time and their bodies cremated. This process took about an hour to an hour and a half. The record for one day, according to Milton Meltzer in *Never to Forget,* is 34,000 people killed and destroyed in 24 hours, through continuous day and night shifts, pg. 130

8. *The Kingdom of Auschwitz* by Otto Friedrich discusses the rats and quotes prisoner Sternberg Newman as saying "the rats would get at the body before it was cold and eat the flesh in such a way that it was unrecognizable before morning." pg. 37.

9. Dr. Olga Lengyel discusses the "mysterious powder" which the Germans put in the food in her book *Five Chimneys,* pg. 95-96.

10. *This Was Oswiecim: The Story of a Murder Camp* by Dr. Filip Friedman, "Documents have been found showing that the "Strem" firm received 112,600 kilo of human bones. They were probably used for soap manufacture. ....We have evidence that there was such a soap factory in Poland." pg. 64.

11. The scope of the research carried on at Auschwitz is well documented in *Auschwitz: A Doctor's Eyewitness Account* by Miklos Nyiszli.

12. Nyiszli talks of forwarding reports and samples to the Berlin Institute marked "War Materials", pg. 134.

13. "The victim had received an injection of chloroform in the heart..." pg. 53. Friedrich also cites that "Mengele....ordered each pair carefully examined and then killed." pg. 56.

14. Both Dr. Nyiszli and Dr. Lengyel confirm this attempt at revolt.

15. Martin Gilbert in his *Atlas of the Holocaust* confirms the massacre of 5,200 Jews at Czernowitz between June 22 and July 16, 1941, pg. 67, map 73.

REFERENCES

Berenbaum, Michael. *The World Must Know.* Boston: Little, Brown and Co. 1993.

Dawidowicz, Lucy. *The War Against the Jews.* New York: Bantam Books. 1984.

Friedman, Filip, Dr. *This was Oswiecim: The Story of a Murder Camp.* London: The United Jewish Relief Appeal. 1946.

Friedrich, Otto. *The Kingdom of Auschwitz.* New York: Harper Perennial. 1994.

Gilbert, Martin. *Atlas of the Holocaust.* New York: William Morrow and Co. 1993.

Lengyel, Olga. *Five Chimneys.* New York: Granada. 1981.

Meltzer, Milton. *Never To Forget: The Jews of the Holocaust.* New York: Harper Collins. 1976.

Mermelstein, Mel. *By Bread Alone.* Huntington Beach, CA.: Auschwitz Study Foundation, Inc. 1979.

Nyiszli, Miklos, Dr. *Auschwitz: A Doctor's Eyewitness Account.* New York: Fawcett Crest. 1960.